These pages are filled with hugely important details, fantastic anecdotes, and practical advice that will be priceless to anyone looking to direct great television.

— J.J. ABRAMS, director of *Star Trek Into Darkness, Star Wars: The Force Awakens, Star Wars: The Rise of Skywalker*, and *Mission: Impossible III*, and creator of *Alias* and *Lost*

Dan Attias has written a book I believe would make any TV director a better director. I wish I had had his book before I ever started.

— DAVID CHASE, creator and showrunner of *The Sopranos*

Dan's writing is reflective of his directing style: sensitive, thoughtful, insightful, and searching. Reading his book, I felt as considered and supported by him as I did when he would direct me within a scene. His account of the culture and process of episodic television is honest and edifying.

— CLAIRE DANES, star of *Homeland* and winner of multiple Emmy awards

I've watched thousands of hours of television, but I can always recognize Dan's work because it is a cut above. If you want to understand what a director does, or would like to be a director, or already are a director and would like to get better at it, or just love television and would enjoy a great series of stories about how it is actually made, stories that will entertain you and make you love television even more — then READ THIS BOOK.

— JOHN LANDGRAF, Chairman of FX Networks and FX Productions

I recommend Dan's generous and much-needed book without reservation. It should be read and studied, certainly by all television directors, but really by all directors.

— JUDITH WESTON, author of *Directing Actors: 25th Anniversary Edition* and *The Film Director's Intuition*

If you are interested in the process, in how it works, or should work, if you want to hear from someone who still finds the fun and the challenge in bringing the story to life, and who has skills up the wazoo, then this man is the one to pay attention to. I did. And it made me better.

— AMY SHERMAN-PALLADINO, creator, co-showrunner, and frequent director of *The Marvelous Mrs. Maisel*

Dan Attias has not only written an incredibly comprehensive guide to directing television, he's written a humanistic and personal memoir of the journey to find the truth through the best storytelling possible and capturing that on film. Speaking from personal experience, Dan is not just a great television director, he's a great director, period. You will love this book.

— NATHAN LANE, icon of the American stage and multiple Tony and Emmy award-winning actor

D1430515

It isn't exaggeration to say that Dan Attias helped build our current golden age of television, one exceptionally crafted hour at a time. I've been directing television for twenty years, and yet every page of this book taught me something I didn't know. No one has Dan's depth of directing experience in such a wide range of genre and tone. He has been one of my most valuable mentors, and I'm thrilled that he is sharing his unique wisdom with the world.

— MATT SHAKMAN, Emmy-nominated director whose credits include *Game of Thrones, Fargo,* and *Succession*

Dan Attias is one of the most talented directors working today, the guy you want directing your most important episode. He has written an essential manual for anyone who wants to understand the craft of television production and directing.

— JOE WEISBERG, creator and co-showrunner of FX's *The Americans,* and JOEL FIELDS, co-showrunner of *The Americans*

Dan Attias has written a brutally honest survival guide for any director of episodic television. Leading us on an engrossingly deep dive into the trenches of the director's world, he writes with great truth and insight about the director's process.

— JOHN BADHAM, director of *Saturday Night Fever, WarGames, Heroes, Nikita, Psych,* and *Supernatural*

A deeply reflective and ingenious award-winning director has given us the gift of this brilliant, in-depth look at the shaping of our human dramas from the inside out, revealing the fundamentals of what "being present" in life entails.

— DANIEL J. SIEGEL, M.D., *New York Times* bestselling author of *Aware, Mind, Brainstorm,* and *Mindsight,* Clinical Professor at the UCLA School of Medicine, and Executive Director of the Mindsight Institute

The chapter on *The Americans* epitomizes who Dan Attias is and magnifies his decades of experience. His gift, mantra, ethos is to continually push, probe, encourage, dive deeper, and ultimately elevate every moment to further the story.

— MATTHEW RHYS, star of *The Americans* and *Perry Mason*

After thirty-five years of thinking I know all there is to know about directing television, Dan swoops in to prove me wrong. I can think of no better book to communicate precisely what this job entails.

— THOMAS SCHLAMME, President of the Directors Guild of America and nine-time Emmy Award–winning director

This is a testament to the joy of storytelling and the infinite power of stories.

— LESLI LINKA GLATTER, executive producer/director of *Homeland,* nominated for eight Emmy awards for directing and winner of three DGA directing awards

Dan approached directing *The Boys* like it was his first job — passionate, dedicated, collaborative, sleeves rolled up, down in the trenches. He is an exceptional artist who never stops working on his craft. With this book, Dan graciously details what he's learned so far.

> — ERIC KRIPKE, creator and showrunner of *The Boys, Supernatural, Timeless,* and *Revolution*

Dan's clear mastery of the art of directing is something every student of the craft should be so lucky to learn from. His years of experience wrestling with challenges inform and elevate the art form — and make for one hell of a great story, not to mention a brilliant career.

> — VEENA SUD, creator and showrunner of *The Killing* and *Seven Seconds* and executive producer of *Cold Case*

The shows that Dan Attias has directed for HBO include *The Sopranos, The Wire, Six Feet Under, Deadwood, Big Love, Treme, Entourage, Hung, True Blood, True Detective* — and these are just his HBO credits. Bringing each of these pieces to the screen was no easy task. He is a master at weaving visually exquisite narratives while also presenting humanity in all its complexity. Dan's love and knowledge for his art are evident in every chapter of this book, which provides a nuanced and expert account of his skills and experiences. It is just as brilliant, insightful, and distinct as Dan's directing.

> — FRANCESCA ORSI, Senior Vice President of Drama Series for HBO

If you want to direct television, then this book is a must for you. Using his wealth of experience, Attias gives you behind-the-scenes access to how many of the best television series are directed.

> — MARX PYLE, MFA, author of *Television on the Wild Wild Web,* adjunct professor at Kentucky Wesleyan University, and co-host of GenreTainment

Dan Attias is a consummate creative force who, in this book, touches on all the aspects of directing and storytelling, inspiring the creative forces within us. His book is authentic, exciting, and boundlessly empowering.

> — DAVE WATSON, author of *Walkabout Undone* and editor of Movies Matter

Being a visiting director on a television series must be one of the oddest leadership positions ever devised, like being asked to run a major corporation just for a few weeks, or temporarily taking over as the lead performer of an established rock band. As a cinematographer who has crossed paths with Dan several times in the past fifteen years, one lesson he has taught me is that one of the director's primary jobs is to quickly spot the difference between phoniness and believability in all aspects of narrative filmmaking. Any filmmaker — novice or experienced — will learn a lot from reading this book.

> — DAVID MULLEN, ASC, cinematographer on *The Marvelous Mrs. Maisel, The Good Wife,* and *Westworld*

On the set of "It's Always Sunny," Dan was tenacious, driven, and able to push us towards making more interesting camera choices that helped build the visual style we still use on the show fifteen years later. A mentor and a friend — I'm forever grateful to his contributions to the show and my life.

    — CHARLIE DAY, co-star and co-showrunner of *It's Always Sunny in Philadelphia*, co-star of *Horrible Bosses*

Anything that's good about my work I've learned from Dan Attias. In this book, he imparts priceless lessons they won't teach you in film school (like how to handle a difficult actor, producer, or deadline). This is one of those books you will read and reread a hundred times, always finding some new flash of insight.

    — MAX JOSEPH, feature and documentary director, and co-star of MTV's *Catfish*

If you are a fan of television, you'll find in Dan's book a fascinating behind-the-scenes peek into the making of your favorite shows from the perspective of a top industry insider. For those of you looking to pursue a career in television directing, the principles, strategies, and stories shared by Dan Attias in these pages will provide guidance and inspiration on your directing journey.

    — STEPH GREEN, Emmy-nominated director whose credits include *The Mandalorian*, *Watchmen*, *The Americans*, *Billions*, and *The Deuce*

In series television, directors usually can't get everything they want. But Dan is able to prioritize telling the story while staying aware of budget concerns and the needs of production. This book offers valuable insights into how he does it and is a "must read" for aspiring directors, as well as anyone else interested in television production.

    — MARK TOBEY, co-executive producer of *Westworld* and assistant director of *True Detective* and *Deadwood*

A treasure trove of practical and creative suggestions, this book is a master class in episodic television directing and understanding the complexity of the many roles that a director needs to know to accomplish their best work.

    — DR. SELISE E. EISEMAN, consultant for colleges on entertainment industry internship programs and former education coordinator for the Directors Guild of America

Dan Attias has years of experience in directing, and he has outlined clearly how to capitalize on the power of story and tell it in the most convincing way. I highly recommend this book.

    — CAROLE DEAN, author of *The Art of Film Funding*

If he had to, Dan Attias could land a television show on the Hudson. A master.

    — HUGH LAURIE, star of *House*, *The Night Manager*, and *Veep*

DIRECTING
GREAT TELEVISION

INSIDE TV'S NEW GOLDEN AGE

DAN ATTIAS

MICHAEL WIESE PRODUCTIONS

Published by Michael Wiese Productions
12400 Ventura Blvd. #1111
Studio City, CA 91604
(818) 379-8799, (818) 986-3408 (FAX)
mw@mwp.com
www.mwp.com

Cover design by Johnny Ink. www.johnnyink.com
Copyediting by Karen Krumpak

Cover photos courtesy Alamy, Allstar Picture Library Ltd.
HBO, Claire Danes, Dominic West, Steve Schirripa,
Michael Imperioli, James Gandolfini, Steven Van Zandt,
and Tony Sirico

Manufactured in the United States of America

Library of Congress Cataloging-in-Publication Data

Names: Attias, Daniel, author.
Title: Directing great television : inside TVs new golden age / Dan Attias.

Description: Studio City, CA : Michael Wiese Productions, [2021] | Summary:
   "Sharing his own process honed over a decades-long career,
   Emmy-nominated director Dan Attias brings you into the actual experience
   of directing series television. Whether it's the high-stakes pressure of
   solving a last-minute problem on set, or the joy of pulling off a
   perfect shot by the skin of your teeth, Attias brings you right into the
   director's chair, sharing his knowledge and taking you through the
   process one challenging episode at a time. Offering a fundamental focus
   on story, and eschewing industry language for plain talk, Attias offers
   in-depth guidance how best to work with actors, how to "speak" through
   the camera, how to work with a showrunner, and how to be ready for the
   many ways a director will be challenged, large and small. Directing
   Great Television is a fascinating window into television's best shows,
   compelling to directors and non-directors alike. Attias's book
   transcends other filmmaking guides by detailing his journey to a
   surprising place of self-discovery, one with applications beyond
   entertainment"-- Provided by publisher.
Identifiers: LCCN 2020056678 | ISBN 9781615933297 (trade paperback)
Subjects: LCSH: Television series--Production and direction.
Classification: LCC PN1992.75 .A88 2021 | DDC 791.4502/32--dc23
LC record available at https://lccn.loc.gov/2020056678

Dedicated to:

The power of stories,

those willing to explore themselves through storytelling,

and my wife, Diana, who has immeasurably enriched my story

TABLE OF CONTENTS

FOREWORD

EVERY SUCCESSFUL TELEVISION SHOW IS A MIRACLE. So many forces conspire against its survival from the very start, and so many hard choices must be made — narrative choices, casting choices, staffing choices, programming choices — any one of which can prove fatal. So it was hardly a surprise to me, walking up the hill behind my house at 5:30 one morning, that everything appeared to be going seriously sideways.

I had been the showrunner of *Homeland* for a little more than four months, and the day before, I had fired exactly half my writing staff, watched a staggeringly disjointed and disappointing cut of the pilot, and learned that the director of the third episode had just dropped out at the last minute. Head down, I was right in the middle of plotting an escape from this train wreck of my own making when I heard a voice:

"Hey, Alex."

I looked up to find my neighbor, Jason Katims, Executive Producer of the hit series *Friday Night Lights* and *Parenthood*. Seeing my agitated state, he asked if I was okay. Well, I told him, not really: "I'm exhausted, paralyzed by the workload, and clearly unfit for the job of running a television show."

At this point, Jason offered the single best piece of advice I've ever received in my career. And it was as ridiculously simple as it was helpful. "Go home," he said, "and get one thing done. Then go into the office and get another thing done. Pretty soon, you'll be on a roll."

So that's what I did. I went straight home, hired Dan Attias to direct the third episode, and — no joke — from that moment on, never looked back.

Dan went on to direct seven more episodes of the show over the next eight years, including "13 Hours in Islamabad" — one of the most intense and emotional hours of *Homeland* ever. There are action sequences in that episode that stand up to the biggest budget feature films and that Dan shot in a single day!

I've often said I don't envy episodic directors. It's a helluva tough job. You're an itinerant laborer, moving from one show to another — each with its own rules and requirements and difficult personalities. You have to be immensely adaptable, relentlessly positive, and the bearer of a very thick skin. Dan Attias is all those things and more; he's a showrunner's dream. No one is better prepared, and no one's preparation better affords them the freedom to improvise on the set. Aside from Dan's technical gifts, which are prodigious, he is especially successful for one reason: He loves his job. A magician with actors and a painter with the camera, Dan has now written a book that teaches us how he does it — an invaluable resource for anyone who wants to be an episodic director, and a flat-out great read for anyone interested in how television is actually made.

Alex Gansa
Showrunner of *HOMELAND*

CHAPTER ONE

WHAT'S UNIQUE ABOUT DIRECTING SERIES TELEVISION?

I AM A DIRECTOR OF SERIES TELEVISION, HAVING directed hundreds of hours of shows you may have watched, from *Miami Vice* (1980s) to *Beverly Hills 90210* (1990s) to *The Sopranos, The Wire, Deadwood,* and *Six Feet Under* (2000s), through *Homeland, The Americans, The Marvelous Mrs. Maisel,* and dozens more. When I was young and just starting out, I was eager to make my mark in cinema. At that time, people didn't take series television very seriously as an artistic form. The television work that came my way felt like practice — a chance to keep active, maybe even learn a little something about directing that I could apply when the next feature came along.

But the surprise for me has been that working in television is where I came of age as a director. TV has offered innumerable opportunities to master my craft and find my creative voice. I was fortunate to be directing during the start of the second so-called "golden age of television" in the late 1990s, a flowering of visually sophisticated and thematically complex series unlike anything that had come before. Thanks to shows like *The Sopranos* and *The Wire,* high-end television now offers more challenges and room to grow than most mass-market films.

Still, a lot of people who get into directing continue to think of film as their goal, and of television as a placeholder until they join directors like Martin Scorsese, Alfonso Cuarón, and Jane Campion in the pantheon. But series television has evolved into its own unique art form, combining the psychological depth of the novel with the allure of the cinema. If you're a director worth your salt, you'll approach the creation of an episode of television with the same care and imagination you would your own film.

From my earliest assignments, I've been privileged to work on many of the shows that helped change the way we see television. In addition to the shows mentioned above, these include *21 Jump Street, Northern Exposure, Party of Five, True Blood, Entourage, Big Love, Treme, Buffy the Vampire Slayer, House, Friday Night Lights, Lost, Alias, Masters of Sex, It's Always Sunny in Philadelphia, The Walking Dead, Damages, Bloodline, Ray Donovan, True Detective, Seven Seconds, The Killing, Get Shorty, Snowfall, Billions,* and *The Boys.* As television has evolved, it's expanded to embrace characters, subjects, and sensibilities that would have been unthinkable before. What we were seeing starting with shows like *The Sopranos, The Wire,* and *Six Feet Under* was the emergence of a new art form.

Television viewers have always enjoyed spending years with characters they love, from Mary Tyler Moore, to the Bunkers, to *Friends* and Jerry Seinfeld. Yet something happened in the late 1990s: Writers and directors began to go deeper and approach their narratives in a more novelistic way. The advantage that novels have always enjoyed over visual forms of storytelling is the depth made possible by the sheer number of hours that readers spend with the characters, like Herman Melville's Captain Ahab or Leo Tolstoy's Anna Karenina. In the '90s, writers and directors began to expand beyond "one off" episodes that kept the world of the show fixed and unchallenged. This led to freedom not simply to recreate the same old favorite character bits but instead to explore characters and dramatic situations with new depth. And viewers loved it. People expanded their conception of what they looked for from television. Binge-watching was born.

In many senses, directing an episode of television and directing a feature film are identical jobs. In both cases, the director bears responsibility for the actors' performances, determines the camera angles, decides how much coverage to shoot, supervises the "director's cut," and must answer innumerable questions from a variety of creative departments. She approves locations and schedule, has critical input on casting choices, and is responsible for taking command of the set. Most importantly, the director in both formats is the one assessing, moment to moment, how the story is working and how best to tell it.

But there are differences. For one, the television script is a given, as opposed to possibly being developed by the director in conjunction with the writer of a feature film. Input can occur, but there generally isn't time for significant changes, and the power balance is heavily weighted toward the episode's writer. This points to the biggest difference between directing features and directing series television: The director in episodic TV must blend his vision with that of the showrunner's, not vice versa. That showrunner, often the writer who created the show, is the one in charge of guiding the writing process, interacting with the network or streaming service, and having significant authority on all creative decisions. It's generally understood that, while the director is empowered in many meaningful ways, the showrunner's vision is the one that everyone serves.

There are other significant differences between feature directing and directing a television episode. Rather than telling a full story from start to finish (and I'm speaking here of "serialized" shows with an ongoing narrative), the episodic director is charged with telling a certain portion of the story, one that needs to reflect on past events and, possibly, foreshadow future ones. She inherits a "visual language" and all the other conventions that have been established by previous episodes. An audience is already invested in the show's story, and their expectations and assumptions must be respected. Whatever deviations you choose to make are experienced *as deviations*, which — if not intentional and done for specific effect — will distract from the story you think you're telling.

Also significant are the time limitations within which the material must be realized. The script is often not given to the director until the day before prep is to start. And television prep time is significantly shorter than for feature films, where eight to fifteen weeks of preparation are common before shooting a ninety-minute to two-hour movie. In television, you get seven or eight days to prepare for filming an hour-long episode. If the script is late, or there are rewrites — or both — rarely is extra time afforded before the train leaves the station. It needs to depart on time because there is another episode following closely behind, and that one can't be delayed, either.

Within the time the director has to prepare for shooting the episode, he is expected to fully absorb the script and develop a vision that embraces the writer's dreams for the material as well as the director's own specific take on it. He must then convey that vision to a battalion of department heads, who may make suggestions to modify or enhance it; however, they cannot properly perform their own preparation without some guidance as to the director's evolving intentions. In addition, the episodic director must offer assurances that she can accomplish everything that is scripted within the time and with the resources available; either that, or she must ask for cuts, more time to shoot, or alternative ways to tell the story — all rolls-of-the-dice with severe consequences if misjudged.

When filming starts, directors of both features and episodic television must deal with the same variables that are part of any day of shooting. (More on that later.) But the bottom line is that the episodic director has far less time to tell the story than a feature director does. And the kicker is that, on high-end television shows these days, viewers expect an episode to look and feel as impressive as those feature films.

As my career in episodic television has progressed, exposing me to a vast range of stories, characters, and perspectives, I'm sometimes reminded of my brief experience in young adulthood as an aspiring actor. Directing is, of course, very different from acting. The director is responsible for telling the entire story, holding the vision that will be realized moment to moment, and being the arbiter, finally, of how it all gets shaped. The director has to see the big picture and steer the journey so that it's one worth taking for the audience. But I can see now that the impulse that led me to acting — to inhabit other roles and discover myself within them — is similar to what appeals to me about directing a wide range of stories and shows. An actor moves from the world of one show to that of another, which means finding oneself in circumstances defined by someone else and needing to accept givens and limitations. Acting involves inhabiting different sensibilities, fitting one's contribution into a larger context, trusting one's instincts in the moment, and making choices. Actors in "improv" companies are advised, when their scene partners introduce new imaginary circumstances, just to say "yes." That sense of acceptance and forward movement with every circumstance that's thrown at you is what directing an episode of television can feel like. Also, just as actors who play classic parts as varied as Lady Macbeth, Willy Loman, and even Batman and Superman have the potential to put their particular stamp on the role, episodic directors are challenged to absorb a "language," as it were, of preexisting characters, environments, and visual cues, and to learn to speak that language in their own voice.

When approached in this way, series directing is an opportunity to enlarge one's experience of life and to discover new depths within oneself. If you're lucky enough to work regularly, and do good work, you'll have the opportunity to immerse yourself in a wide variety of imaginary worlds, discovering insights probably unavailable to you anywhere else. And, because the process is so collaborative, you will find others to contribute to your efforts and inspire you in ways that enrich your work and your experience.

The episodic director often labors in obscurity, usually unrecognized for the creative contributions she has made. But to do the best job you're capable of, you must take responsibility for the storytelling, making the words on the page come alive. You must accept all of the sometimes-onerous limitations, foreswear too much whining about setbacks (even those for which you might not have been responsible), and be okay with not getting the ego strokes you'll probably feel you deserve for a job well done. But when you do pull it off and create something beautiful and entertaining, it's a fantastic feeling. In my experience, it does not happen without frustration, roadblocks, fear of failure, and confronting all of one's own insecurities and self-doubts. The best way through, for me, is to recognize that the master we must serve is not our ego but the story, for we have an opportunity to connect meaningfully with those viewers who will accompany us on the journey of the tale.

As you may have guessed, episodic directing is an art form I have grown to love and respect. If it's something at which you hope to excel, or even if it's something you're curious about because you love the medium, I hope the insights I share in these pages will give you a clear idea of what comes with the territory. This book is my way of pointing you toward where issues may arise, how solutions might reveal themselves, and how a mindset dedicated to story can lead you to the truest expression of your vision.

This isn't a traditional "how to" book. It's not that I don't have pointers — I do. I have stories. I have battle scars. I've made mistakes. I've had breakthroughs. I've seen what works and what doesn't. But more crucially, I've gotten to know what works best for me in putting myself in service of story. I hope, through reading about my experiences, you'll find the tools that lead you to discover your best directing self, too.

I've always appreciated what John Wells (who as showrunner of the series E.R. spearheaded its groundbreaking first couple of seasons) is said to have advised young directors about the job: "Make it feel just like an episode of E.R., only better." If that "only better" both thrills you and keeps you up at night, you might just be cut out for this job.

CHAPTER TWO

THE SCHOOL OF HARD KNOCKS

THERE'S NO REAL TRAINING FOR THE EXPERIENCE of stepping onto the hurtling train that is an episodic television show. Neither film school, nor having written a script, nor anything else I can think of really prepares you. You need a talent for storytelling for sure, but in addition to that, you need to learn how to deal with those times when you don't know the answers. That will involve collaborating with those who can help carry your unique vision through the whole, difficult process, which at times may feel like it's conspiring against you. On top of all this, you're called upon to lead and have command.

If anyone has transitioned to this job seamlessly without making errors of consequence, I'd like to meet them.

I learned a good deal about directing from getting an M.F.A. in film production, then working as a trainee assistant director before becoming second assistant director for Francis Coppola, Steven Spielberg, and Wim Wenders, among others. My first opportunity to direct professionally was a feature film, and I felt like I was on my way to making my mark as a director. But it was not until I actually started my directing career in series television that I appreciated the unique challenges of this format. There is nothing quite like showing up on your first shooting day and being responsible, generally within the first fifteen or twenty minutes, for directing the rehearsal, staging the scene, and working out the camera positions. Plus, you know that should you change your mind later about the decisions you're making, you will jeopardize completing the rest of the day's work.

You're going to misstep, and you're going to make mistakes. Not only will there be errors of execution in which your choices create production inefficiencies or story problems, you'll also be likely to stumble interpersonally, offending someone either by not understanding their process or by your own unconsciousness of how you're presenting yourself. Few situations require dealing with such immediate and potentially challenging feedback as how you, the one in command, relate to other people who are also trying to survive and thrive in a competitive industry. Part of your own learning curve will be developing an ability to express yourself intelligently and responsibly amid the pressures of the moment. Ready or not, you're in a position of authority and have it in your power to deeply impact other people and the project itself, positively or negatively, by acts of commission or omission.

In short, no one can really be prepared for all the personal and professional challenges that this job involves without having had some experience. Even then, no matter how much experience you've had, there will always be new challenges for which you won't be prepared. Learning can be painful — especially if you don't accept the reality that missteps are part of the journey.

One of my first TV directing assignments was an episode in the third season of *Miami Vice* entitled "Baby Blues." I felt during it (and after, frankly) like I'd received a pummeling. I was unprepared for several things, some of which I couldn't have foreseen and others I should have.

I'd been hired for the job because I qualified as "a feature director," my first directing job having been the feature film *Stephen King's Silver Bullet*. It's rare now for TV producers to automatically assume that feature directors bring added value to an episode of television. As I'll explore later in these pages, there are some different skills that are required of episodic directing, and at the time, I certainly hadn't developed them.

The creative force behind *Miami Vice*, the quintessential police show of the mid-1980s, was Michael Mann, its executive producer. At this point in the life of the series, Mann was more involved with feature-film projects and was mostly absent from production, though he retained ultimate oversight. This awkward configuration led to some dysfunction in the decision-making process, as Mann was consulted sometimes later than he should have been, and his input could send the production team scrambling. As events unfolded, I developed the distinct impression that nearly everyone was looking for scapegoats to blame for any perceived missteps. As an example of the sorts of problems that could arise, the leading guest role we needed to cast was for an adoption attorney, whose schtick in his televised advertisements was to portray a bumbling and endearing clown. He would prance and posture, promising to bring happiness to couples seeking to adopt by providing them with children from around the world. In a clever misdirect, he was also the central villain of the episode, revealed as being a cynical and sociopathic kidnapper of babies from third-world mothers. After an actor was found who could credibly pull off the fumbling clown persona and we had begun shooting, Mann belatedly mandated that this character, the central adversary for the episode, should instead be a cool, slickly villainous character. The script was hastily reconceived to erase any mention of clowns, and I was stuck with an actor completely wrong for the role.

Of more consequence was that the on-location producer with me in Miami, to whom I'd been conveying my plans and intentions, wasn't communicating any of my concerns to the creative team in Los Angeles. The first time I became aware of this was after shooting the episode's backstory in a scene establishing the kidnapping of an infant from his Colombian mother. It had been written to take place in a peasant village, ransacked by the attorney's henchmen, who chase down the mother and wrest away her child. When it became clear that no such village existed anywhere near Miami, and that the budget could not accommodate creating an entire community, I suggested an alternative: We could have the kidnapping take place on a country road, where we might establish a ramshackle bus transporting Colombian peasants. The kidnappers could create a roadblock and board the front of the bus, while the child's mother, clutching her baby, could sneak out the rear exit and flee across a field. The kidnappers would give chase and brutally snatch the child from her. The producer on location approved, and we shot the sequence.

When the dailies were screened in Los Angeles the following day, the altered staging was a surprise to the L.A. producers, including the writer of the episode, who may well have been in damage control after having disappointed Mann about the lead villain. I gathered that he had now become alarmed that I was out of my lane and would do further damage to his original concept, perhaps further tarnishing him. At this point, I made a neophyte's mistake: I misread a detail that took place in a scene in which a bound and gagged victim was transferred from the trunk of one car to another. I mixed up the two vehicles from what the script had indicated, so the transfer occurred in the opposite direction. Though it made story sense in a different way from what the writer intended, I admittedly hadn't read the sequence carefully enough, and my error made me a fair target for anyone looking to shift blame in case the episode turned out to be disappointing.

Soon enough, I felt the vibe of being mistrusted, learning, for example, that I had been criticized for a prop I selected for the child who was snatched from his mother and who was now two years old. The script required him to cry on cue to convey to his birth mother (the Colombian peasant, who risks her life to come in search of him in Miami) that heroically she ought to leave the boy with his adoptive parents, who have now cared for him for two years and to whom he is now completely attached. To prepare for this moment, I had spent a weekend afternoon with the child we'd cast and his real-life parents. They let me borrow his "transitional object," a smallish white piece of material that I thought might produce the desired emotional reaction if it were taken from him at the moment of separation — which, if I remember correctly, it did. I had been concerned with getting a performance from a two-year-old, but the fact that the prop wasn't more expensive or colorful led to my taste becoming suspect in the eyes of the producers.

My biggest challenge, however, was that I was still very new to "film language" — not just the stylistic idiosyncrasies of this particular show, but the basic grammar of film editing, including what shots might be required to edit a scene effectively. I had made shot lists reflecting my ideas for how most scenes would be edited, but when lead actor Don Johnson — then known as the "King of Miami" and famous for taking over the set — "suggested" changes to the way I'd planned to shoot, I felt like a deer in the headlights. I was the newcomer, both to the show and to the job itself. I'd felt unsure of my plan to begin with, so usually I acceded to his ideas because, frankly, I thought they were better. My self-esteem plummeted, I felt unsupported from every quarter, and I asked myself why on earth I would ever want to put myself in this position again.

My spirits lifted once I got into the editing room and saw the ways my choices had worked, despite the lack of support or encouragement and my own battered confidence. The performances were good, all the dramatic moments had been delivered, and my camera angles effectively told the story. But I knew it was unlikely I'd ever be rehabilitated in the eyes of the producers because I had become a lightning rod for all their projected fears and an easy scapegoat for anyone seeking cover. I later learned that the writer of this episode, in his notes on my director's cut, expressed surprise that the show had worked as well as it had, particularly since it must have succeeded in spite of the director. Self-serving as his comment may have been, it also was an early lesson to me that sometimes even writers have little idea of what the director actually does.

When, several months later, I got my next job — again on a show with good ratings and a substantial following — I was determined to be better prepared and to communicate more effectively. The show was *Beauty and the Beast*, a 1987 contemporary update of the fairytale. By chance, the particular episode I was hired to direct, entitled "Labyrinths," dealt with subjects that touched me personally. I had been reading about rites of passage into adulthood and had spent time with poet Robert Bly and mythologist Michael Meade, who were exploring ways our culture has been deficient in providing male initiation experiences for young men. I don't recall how it was that the showrunner knew of my interest in those subjects, but, even before my prep period began, he engaged with me animatedly about the episode and invited me to share my thoughts and insights on how we might sharpen the episode's focus around those themes. He seemed truly happy for the dovetailing of his interests with mine.

I was a fan of the show and excited to work on it. But, because I had been unsure of the visual choices I'd made on my last job and had to endure the ignominy of being unable to defend them, I was determined to create a plan and a visual scheme in which I could fully believe. I wanted to be the authority on set, to tell the story the way I saw it. The only way I could figure out how to do that was to deepen myself as the storyteller, to fully immerse myself in the story, and to find my own authentic response to the material.

One of the challenges in beginning a directing career is that there really aren't intermediate stages at which you take on some duties before easing your way into others, the way in the restaurant world people may ascend from prep cook, to line cook, to sous chef, to chef de cuisine. With directing, you go from having none of the responsibility to having all of it. With *Miami Vice*, I'd embraced the concept of "fake it till you make it" when presenting myself to the crew. In some situations in life, there's logic to this strategy, which can get you through turbulent times full of crisis and self-doubt. But where it becomes dangerous is if you forget you've been faking it when you should be figuring out the "making it" part. On *Miami Vice*, I'd dealt with my shortcomings, inexperience, and lack of confidence by simply hoping for the best. On this new job, I was determined to be prepared when shooting began and admit to myself how unprepared I felt on so many creative questions that needed answers.

In the past, I'd treated my lack of expertise as a dirty little secret that, to acknowledge, would be to subject myself to fierce judgment (my own included). That approach was childish. But more importantly, it was ineffective. The best directing is a creative act, and creativity, I've come to understand, starts with curiosity, with *not knowing*. Everyone, of course, has an ego and some concern for how they appear to others. But if you lead with that, you will cut yourself off from making discoveries and from your own inner resources. Instead, you will protect your own, fragile self-image either by making safe, predictable choices and not risking mistakes or, as I had done on my previous job, by pretending even to yourself that you know more than you do. The fact is that with episodic directing, the end result will be judged on its merits. Your best chance at success is to overcome self-deception and let curiosity lead you through the questions for which you need answers. Thus my new strategy became to admit that, for many important questions, I hadn't a clue.

At another time, in another place, I had come upon a similar challenge, but without such pressure to perform. I was in graduate film school in a critical-studies program, which I'd only enrolled in so that I could take the acting classes the department offered. As part of the curriculum, students had to make a short film. (In those days, it was on Super 8 film stock.) I wrote a short script, gathered some acting friends, directed it, then took the raw footage to the editing room. I hadn't much of an idea how to proceed, but as I played with assembling the footage, I saw that joining two pieces of film would create in me an immediate response. The way I could know what story was getting communicated (and what emotions or ideas were evoked) was by paying attention to what was happening inside myself. I could shape the viewer's experience by carefully monitoring my own — piecing together all the elements until they drew from me precisely the feelings or thoughts I wanted the audience to have at each moment of the storytelling. Yet somehow, years later, I had forgotten to rely on my own sensitivities and had gotten lost in trying to look like I knew what I was doing. The limitations of that approach had just been made painfully clear to me.

On *Beauty and the Beast,* though I feared being regarded as a novice who needed extra time to figure things out, I asked the production staff if I might have access to the soundstage on the weekend. I committed to staying with each problem and taking as long as necessary to plan my staging and camera angles, even if it meant working through the night. Because I was by myself, I felt no pressure to have quick answers. I made it a point to absorb every feature of the set environments, almost as if they had become characters themselves in the story. I made it my intention to test each visual idea using my own senses: How did a particular image strike me? What feeling or subjective state was I experiencing? Staying patient and curious, I noticed where my attention was drawn and what images I felt invited to see. This began an inquiry that led to camera moves, to key visual moments, and, at last, to a plan.

Through having trained as an actor, I already felt well-versed in getting to the emotional and dramatic heart of a scene. But being on the actual set, free of distractions, I imagined inhabiting each role and developed ideas for movement based on character intention and what the location offered. If one part of the set had greater visual interest than another, I thought about how things might be staged to take advantage of that. My bias is always to seek character-appropriate behavior, even if it means having to sacrifice a particular visual image. But with a little imagination, I found it not too difficult to have the best of both: compelling visuals and appropriate action.

More questions arose: How could I frame a particular character's coverage to take advantage of a background that might give context to their words and actions? Are they shy, avoiding stimulation? If so, would it be better to see only a bare wall behind them? Or are they fully engaged with the world, drawn to bustle and excitement? A background vibrant with activity might be the best choice for their angle so the audience can associate them with those qualities. Interestingly, in real life, people drawn to activity, or those who are shy, would likely choose to place themselves in the opposite position so that they might look at what gives them comfort. But in film language, it's often more important to consider what a visual cue might stimulate in the viewer.

I considered what I wanted to see as each beat of the story unfolded. If I'd imagined an actor walking toward the lens and away from her scene partner while he's talking, I asked myself, would I like her to approach into a strong, foreground close-up, commanding focus? Or would it be better to frame her just grazing the lens so that focus might be thrown back to the actor speaking? Is it the listener's response or the speaker we should be interested in at that moment?

In identifying what was important to me, a visual plan began to emerge for which I could take full responsibility, because it was in service to the story I was telling. There was no "correct" camera angle, there was only what I wanted to see, what subjective state I wished my viewers to inhabit, and where I wanted to direct their attention.

Camped out on the sets of *Beauty and the Beast*, I was reminded of my early insights from film school. What was important was how I *perceived*. My own sensory response was the barometer on which I would rely. I needn't worry about anything other than how I wanted to experience the story. I challenged myself to dig deeply into what brought the story alive for me, because if I weren't fully engaged, how could I possibly expect to engage the audience?

It was exhilarating. I took responsibility for every moment being communicated, measuring whether or not it was credible and sustained my interest. If I had an idea that could not be implemented because a necessary prop or set piece wasn't there, I could ask that it be added before the scene was scheduled to shoot. If I saw that by removing a wall I could place the camera to provide a better visual context through which to view the performance, I could make sure the wall was made "wild," meaning it could be removed when shooting away from it but replaced for the reverse angle.

I took responsibility by defining what was important in each scene and targeting the significant moments. I chose camera moves on the basis of how they made me feel. Did they create the appropriate subjective state? Or did they call attention to themselves and distract from the story? If so, I would reject them. Rather than trying to think of what the "correct" or "cinematic" camera angle was, I turned my attention to how I wanted to see the scene unfold. What visual choices would enhance what I was trying to create and point the audience to the richest possible experience?

It turns out that rather than being something to fear, the ability to empty oneself, to "not know," can be empowering. But it takes nerve and courage. In the pressure cooker of series-television production, it's important to find a quiet center within yourself where you can be totally open and receptive. It's most likely from that state that you'll be able to perceive the small detail, the precise moment in the script, or even just the feeling that can point you to the story that is yours to discover and to tell.

Armed with a much deeper connection to the material, I was better prepared to take advantage of the help available to me in the form of director of photography, production designer, assistant director, and all the other departments. Being able to convey a vision and a plan enabled me to invite their contributions for how the episode might be enhanced. I had taken ownership of the story.

But a painful lesson was yet to come.

I started shooting, and it could not have gone better. The episode was about a teenage boy undergoing an initiatory experience that liberated him from his dependency on an overbearing father. The young man had run away into "the underworld" — abandoned subway tracks beneath New York City — where "the beast" (Ron Perlman), a kind of half-lion, half-man, presided over a subculture of society's outcasts. He was the series hero and romantic partner to "the beauty" (Linda Hamilton), and he had mythic stature. One sequence I created was a montage of several characters sharing with the teenager their experiences in this secret place and how what they'd learned had strengthened them enough to meet life's challenges. I wanted the feeling of a different dimension of time, with each of these characters speaking to the boy from a deep place within themselves, unaffected by everyday concerns. The camera floated by each of them, dissolving from one to the other in dreamlike fashion, as if the boy was absorbing the teaching deep within his psyche. The response I got from the producers was overwhelming. The showrunner said he'd never seen dailies as beautiful or as moving.

The next day, I got a performance from the featured guest star that led to the entire crew bursting into applause after his last take, a performance I had helped him reach by not cutting the camera after he'd completed the dialogue. I encouraged him to begin the scene again right away from the freed emotional state he had reached by the scene's end, which propelled his performance into previously unexplored territory. It was riveting. More praise and delight from the producers. By the third or fourth day in an eight-day schedule, I was approached to see if I would direct the episode that started prep immediately after mine finished. The showrunner told me it was the most important episode of the season, and I was the director he most trusted.

I was thrilled, of course, but because it overlapped with a major holiday, I needed to check with my family to see if they'd mind altering some of our plans. My wife made it work, and on the next day, the deal was sealed.

Then, on about the sixth or seventh day, I noticed that something had seriously changed. I stopped getting feedback from the producers. They also became noticeably curt with me on the phone. I could not for the life of me understand it. I thought we were still getting terrific work, and I was particularly excited about the themes the showrunner had encouraged me to explore in our initial conversations.

On the second-to-last day, the showrunner called me, expressing unhappiness bordering on anger. I had not, he told me, shot a close-up of one of the actors (the young man's father) in a climactic scene. I explained that there was still time to grab it if he felt it necessary, but that the reason I hadn't shot it was that I thought cutting to it would be a distraction from the story we were telling. We had agreed in prep that this would be a story about a teenage boy moving toward ritual adulthood by finding the true *father within*, personified by Ron Perlman's "beast." Part of separating from his smothering father involved a key initiatory challenge, which was to develop an aptitude for containment: the ability to keep a vital secret. In this case, it meant not telling anyone about the existence of this underworld because that would lead to its being destroyed. When the boy resurfaces and is hugged by his father, with legions of police and firemen who'd been searching for him standing by, Linda Hamilton's character watches off to the side, hoping the young man will not reveal the existence of the sacred world down below. The story to me was in the look between Linda Hamilton and the boy while he is still in the embrace of his father. The look conveys to her that he will not be swept up in all the emotion and betray their shared secret. I saw no reason to cut to a close-up of the father because it would undercut the moment; the father's emotions were not relevant at this point. But I sensed the showrunner felt strongly about it, so we brought the actors back on the last day to recreate the parent's close-up.

When I finished the last day, I went to the line producer to ask where and when I should report to start prepping the following episode. He said that there might be a change of plans, and that I should report to the showrunner's office the next day. I pointed out that I had already adjusted my own schedule and would like more information. But he said nothing more than for me to show up at the showrunner's suite the next afternoon. I felt a little like I was being summoned to the principal's office. That proved to be an understatement.

If you've seen the movie *Network* and the scene in which Howard Beal (Peter Finch) is called into the conference room to see the producer (Ned Beatty), you'll have some idea of what I went through. The showrunner sat across from me, a scowl on his face, his line producer and co-executive producer on a sofa. I still recall his opening line: "I was seduced by your beautiful style, and you f****d me."

I sat there, flabbergasted. He then went on to tell me how I'd "subverted" his show, as if he'd never signed off on the approach we'd discussed. He said that the heart of the show was emotion, and that I was obviously incapable of eliciting it. That was something I'd never been accused of, it being the one strong suit of which I was sure. Incredulous, I asked if he had watched the scene during which the crew was so moved, they had burst into applause.

"Oh, well, you can handle the darker emotions, but not the tender ones."

I came to realize that this man had created a hit whose appeal often rested on its romantic escapism. I understood the romance. But I had been handed a storyline that dramatized something different: a brutal father's failure to appreciate his imaginative son, and the son's developing the strength to move forward in life by finding an "inner" father to bless him. I had worked hard so that this story would not be at the expense of the romance between the main regular characters, but might in fact strengthen that relationship by the surrogate roles they played together in the young man's journey.

It seemed to me that this showrunner had gotten cold feet about the episode and was having second thoughts about the wisdom of doing it at all. Showrunners are under tremendous pressure, and there is a great difference between having a hit — getting well-paid and being something of a star yourself — and being among the throngs of mostly anonymous writers hoping to get a project off the ground. If a show gets canceled, the experience can be like dropping instantly from the penthouse to the basement. Whether or not that played into his worry that the show was deviating too much from its pattern, he now wanted what seemed to me a purely sentimental story, the opposite of everything we'd discussed.

He even impugned my motives, accusing me of having deliberately subverted some of the show's signature visual moments. I asked which, and he cited a lighting effect that occurred whenever a character entered the underworld of the subway tunnels. A high-intensity lamp was aimed straight down through a skylight to mimic sunlight, and characters entering the tunnel would disappear into the extremely bright light.

I was disappointed that the producer who had been on set that day and who was sitting there opposite the showrunner did not mention the truth of what had occurred: The high-intensity lamp had malfunctioned. It could still throw a beam of light, but if our young hero stepped within it, the light was not intense enough to make him disappear from view. We faced either not filming and having to come back at considerable expense another time, or shooting a version I proposed, which might disguise the fact that the light effect was missing. I suggested that if we see the beam of light as the teenager approaches and, just before he enters it, cut back to Linda Hamilton's character watching him disappear (as viewers of the show would assume he had) we might salvage the schedule. If it didn't work, I suggested, we'd still be in the same boat of having to schedule it for another time. But the showunner seemed unwilling even to consider reassessing my intention.

This went on for forty-five minutes, after which he informed me that I would not be directing the next episode. I told him that I was sorry he was so unhappy and that I hoped his opinion would change once he saw my cut. It didn't feel like the time to mention that we had a deal memo in place for me to work on the next episode, so he would either have to pay me for it or face Directors Guild arbitration. He would later find himself on the short end of that arbitration, which did little to assuage my sense of being wronged. But he basically disassembled my director's cut, eviscerating my carefully crafted visual design so that he might make the show as conventional as possible. He eliminated as much edge as he could in the conflict between father and son, and he cut into my elegant opening shot, which visually defined the show's themes, dramatic focus, and protagonist. In doing so, he obscured any sense of the focus we had discussed for the story.

I was hugely disappointed and felt horribly treated. But worse, I didn't know whether or not I'd ever work again. Here was yet another experience from which I could reasonably assume there would be no good references for future employment; more likely, they would be devastating. I was challenged to my core to fathom how things could have changed so quickly. I felt I had "found" myself on this episode, discovered my voice and a way of working that might (and did) serve me in my future efforts. Yet it had all crashed and burned, even as I felt I had arrived at my calling. I had tasted the exhilaration of being able to access my inner resources, putting them in service to the deeper underpinnings of the story. And I had connected with the cast and crew, sharing a vision that inspired them to contribute creatively. But the show would never be seen in its intended form, and I might be deprived of another opportunity.

It took many months before I was presented with that next opportunity, and it arrived with an amusing asterisk. The offer came from a showrunner who had once been on staff at *Beauty and the Beast*. He reported to me that he had been subjected to nearly identically harsh accusations from that showrunner and had seen others similarly accused. He wasn't worried about anything said about me from that experience, and I felt greatly relieved.

The new show, entitled *Wolf*, was an interesting one. I applied many of the things I had learned from my previous experience, prepping thoroughly and letting the story seep deeply into my bones. The first few days of shooting went well enough, I thought. On the third day, as I was walking to the set, I checked my phone messages and heard this from the producer/director: "The dailies are fantastic! We couldn't be happier. Your footage is beautiful, and the performances are great."

As soon as I clicked off, I immediately said to myself, "Boy, am I glad I had the experience on *Beauty and the Beast* so I know not to take any of *that* seriously." And I stopped in my tracks. Had I just said I was *glad* for that long, nightmarish experience? Was I really now able to be grateful for lessons learned and actually feel *stronger* for having gone through it? Apparently so.

What I was glad for was that I had a new relationship to my work. I knew to rely on my own sense of things and to not be quite so dependent on the judgment of others. We all enjoy approval, and I certainly wasn't through with wanting that. But now I understood that, despite their lofty position, showrunners are still human. How they respond to personal and career pressures — how effective they are as leaders — will vary from one individual to the next. If the producers of *Wolf* had had a negative response, I would have asked where they were unhappy and how I might address the problems. But I felt I would be less thrown if something went askew in the communication between us, more skilled at preventing that from happening, and better able not to take personally reactions I felt I did not deserve.

I have since gone on to work with a wide variety of showrunners, each unique in their own way. Almost always, they've been wonderful, creative people. In my relationship to each of them, I try to understand, as much as I can, their vision for the show they've created or are supervising. I want to learn the deeper questions that interest them and the particular hopes they have for how they will be explored. It has been a great blessing in my life to have worked with so many gifted people who invite me into their sensibility and who open me to deeper aspects of myself.

As time has passed and the sting from *Beauty and the Beast* has abated, I can see more clearly the real value of that experience. It was what I learned in prep, before things ever blew up: the importance of taking full responsibility for every story point that gets communicated, and the opportunity we as directors have to bring ourselves to the telling. I learned the value of sensing into a story and imagining its twists and turns as fully as possible until it becomes *my* story to tell. Now, I do not rest in my prep period until I feel I have discovered every possible nuance within the script and what I need to do to communicate it. I understand there will be more to discover during shooting. But being thoroughly prepared increases your capacity to be creative on the set. It gives you the confidence to stay open to new ideas — your own and others' — and puts you in a better position to evaluate whether or not they enrich the story.

When young directors shadow me on a job, I encourage them, before they ever see how I solve staging or camera challenges, to make a plan of their own. Until you face the blank page, you won't discover what good directing really entails: a willingness to face the void of "not knowing" and to explore choices. This is true not only in prep, but throughout the whole creative process. Sometimes, only by being able to tolerate making "bad" choices (equivalent to a writer's poor first draft) can you find your way to the good ones. Sensing for yourself what works and what doesn't can be a painstaking process. Finally arriving at what feels right is the first step in making your story come alive, and it anchors you to something that can take root. Ultimately, your job is not just to serve the showrunner, but also to honor your sense of what's true and your own instincts for what makes a story worth telling.

CHAPTER THREE

CREATING THE WORLD OF YOUR STORY

O NE OF THE CHALLENGES IN STORYTELLING OF any kind is how to create context, which the dictionary defines as "the circumstances that form the setting for an event, statement, or idea, and in terms of which it can be fully understood and assessed." Essentially, context is the world out of which a story emerges. The story is suggested by the script, but the outcome depends upon how the script is realized. As director, you're charged not only with fleshing it out, but with breathing life into it as well. It's important to acquaint your audience with the world it's entering — the rules and conventions — so that when key dramatic or comedic moments occur, viewers will have the necessary information to understand them.

As director, you know far more about every moment in the story than your audience does. It's easy to misjudge how the story will land if you assume knowledge the viewers may not yet have. They only know what you "tell" them or allow them to infer. So it's a good idea to remember always to be part audience yourself in the telling. Something might not work simply because the audience doesn't have the proper frame of reference. There are, of course, instances in which keeping the audience in the dark works to your advantage — in setting up suspense or springing a surprise reveal, for example. But that is something you want to *choose*, and those strategies work best when you're aware of how you're manipulating context.

I once directed an episode about a teenage boy who sought in fantasy the sorts of adventures he longed for in real life. An overbearing father devalued the boy's imagination, which was his real strength. The boy regularly played Dungeons & Dragons with his friends, and the script opened with a game in progress. The scene established how the boy saw his life as an adventure in which imagination could help him navigate his difficulties. So I asked the propmaster to find the most detailed, intricately designed King and Queen game pieces. I also asked the camera department to order "macro" lenses, which can focus on small objects at very close range, making them appear large.

The shot I designed to begin the episode started "inside" the D&D board on a close-up of the King, then pulled back to the Queen and revealed that neither she nor the King were life-sized, but were, in fact, miniature figurines. The camera pulled back farther, tilting up to the face of a boy announcing his move. It continued its pullout to show four boys positioned around the board, one after another taking their turns. It then panned to one boy in particular and began pushing in on him. This boy, the hero of the story, conceives an inventive, very imaginative move, which wins the game; the shot ends on *his* close-up, bookending the shot with the close-up opening image of the King.

What I hoped to accomplish with this lengthy shot was not only to introduce the hero in dramatic fashion, but also to establish his world: imagination itself. I wanted to put the viewer inside that imagination by starting close on the King figurine. Then, by framing all the boys within a single shot rather than cutting to a close-up of each as he spoke, I hoped to make clear that the boy we should be interested in was the one on whom the shot pushed in. I did shoot close-ups of the other teens to be used later in the scene; however, my plan was to let the audience be carried by the one continuous shot until it arrived at its main subject. The framing and movement of the camera put the audience first into a subjective experience of the D&D fantasy world, and then into the imagination of the one boy in particular. In mirroring the opening shot on the King, the closing image tied the two together, under-lining the boy's fascination with this particular fantasy figure.

It would have been possible, of course, not to have such an elabo-rate and time-consuming opening shot and simply to cut to each boy as he said his line. Presumably, the audience would under-stand that these are boys who enjoy playing games that involve their imagination. The viewers might also have understood that the hero was the one with the elegant solution. Those story points probably would have been delivered. But the *felt* experience would not have been the same. The viewers would not have been as involved with the world of the game, nor as intrigued by the subjective experience of the episode's hero. Moreover, the visual tie-in with the King announced a theme of the story that the episode would explore.

These are the areas in which you as director can make a difference, and they generally are not written in the script. The director's job is to determine what story you're telling, and then to commit all available resources to telling it in the most effective way possible. As a storyteller, I sometimes feel my job is akin to sitting around a campfire at night surrounded by dense forest, telling a story under a starlit sky, faces reflecting the glow of a flickering flame. In that setting, your audience would probably be very receptive to a good scary story. Yet imagine the different challenges you would face telling the same story in a bright, fluorescent-lit room. What narrative devices would you have to invent to recreate the same emotional space as that of the nighttime forest? Snoopy in the old *Peanuts* comic strips wasn't the first to begin his stories with "It was a dark and stormy night." Hackneyed and overused, perhaps, but it creates context — and it does so fast.

Comedy is often dependent on seeming to establish one context, only to shift unexpectedly to another. Reframing a conventional context into something else can challenge taboos and expose truths about human nature. *It's Always Sunny in Philadelphia*, a hilarious show centering on some of the worst-behaved characters imaginable, offers the vicarious fun of a world where nearly all the characters are self-absorbed and narcissistic. The show would be far less funny if the characters had no awareness that they were violating moral conventions. Their choices are funnier and more outrageous because of the added context that they know the right thing to do but choose not to do it, then indulge in tortured justifications for why they invariably do the "wrong" thing.

In a first season episode entitled "Underaged Drinking: A National Concern," the bar run by this group of malingerers — Paddy's Pub — is attracting little business. In one scene, the characters riff hilariously on how much more income they would bring in if they were to serve alcohol to minors. They make the decision to do so, and unbridled chaos soon ensues. But during the rehearsal process, something felt missing to me (again, the question always to ask yourself is "How does this make me feel?").

The missing element, I realized, was one of the hallmarks of that creative team's brilliant humor, and I suggested that they take a beat to consider, then reject the idea of serving minors as morally reprehensible and obviously something they should not do. In the final cut of the show, after a pause in which each character briefly acknowledges that this is truly an irresponsible idea, their greed reasserts itself. They begin to argue, with tortured logic, why it would actually be morally *correct* to open the bar to minors. The character Mac (Rob McElhenney) completely flips the argument: "Maybe we have a social *responsibility* to provide a safe haven for these kids to be kids!" The need to convince themselves establishes the context, which is that they have no business even considering serving minors. It becomes not just funny but spotlights a truth, even an amusing cautionary tale, about how human nature can so cleverly lead us astray.

Among the great developments in this current "golden age" of television are the many excellent shows that give viewers the opportunity to watch, and often identify with, morally compromised or flawed characters who struggle with many of the challenges we ourselves face. By creating a context in which we can recognize ourselves in morally compromised characters — characters who share our own longings and disappointments — these shows put audiences in a position to reconsider simple, reassuring assumptions about themselves — assumptions that might be, to some degree, naïve or disingenuous.

In *The Sopranos*, for example, it might be easy to dismiss Tony Soprano's all-too-human foibles and moral compromises by pigeonholing him as simply a mobster. Yet by also establishing him as a family man, the context becomes more complicated, as does our response to his transgressions. One of the great conflicts in the series is Tony's relationship with his mother, Livia. When directing the second episode ("46 Long") of the show's first season, I was handed a storyline in which Tony (James Gandolfini) has to make the decision to move Livia (Nancy Marchand) into an assisted living facility, despite her virulent objections. The script detailed Tony's stress in handling the demands of business and family while simultaneously trying to be a caring son to his sociopathic mother. In one of the opening sequences, he is at the strip club he owns, juggling a business crisis, a request from his wife to find their son's middle-school teacher's stolen car, and pressure to check in with his mother, who misses no opportunity to guilt-trip him for his inattention. The pilot episode had established that Tony was experiencing panic attacks, and this scenario was giving us an opportunity to understand just why he might be susceptible to them. To properly establish that context, it would be necessary to create the sense that Tony was being bombarded from all sides and that his stress was considerable.

In working with the cast, I wanted to make sure that each character who approached Tony with a problem to solve felt entitled to his attention and was oblivious to any of Tony's other responsibilities. There was humor in the fact that in trying to please him, they were actually profoundly irritating him since their very presence kept him from his work. Keeping the pacing up-tempo was critical to conveying Tony's tension in having to handle so much at once. James Gandolfini did a masterful job of embodying a man managing, barely, to stay ahead of each curve — until he takes a phone call from his mother. She is the show-stopping centerpiece of the sequence.

I considered how best to establish the complexity of Tony's emotions as he deals with her confounding presence in his life and in his psyche. I knew there were opportunities in the setting, especially if the seductive, nude dancers were seen moving provocatively in the background, as if summoning the primal feminine energy that Livia activates in him, keeping him guilt ridden and subconsciously enthralled. I chose a wide-angle lens to shoot Tony's close-up during their phone call, enabling the camera to include the naked women behind his head, as if they exist in the back of his psyche. I hoped this would create an association for the viewer, suggesting Tony's unconscious enslavement to powerful feminine forces. Without that sort of context, I believe the overall impact of the scene would have been less provocative and substantial. And it was delivered because I created visual connections that were not specifically indicated in the script: Livia's place in Tony's psyche was contextualized and made more interesting.

It's always worth asking how you might deepen or enrich the context you establish for a particular moment; it can affect the overall power of your scene or story. In a great show like *The Wire*, these kinds of opportunities are especially rich. I directed a final season episode entitled "Transitions," which dramatizes the changing circumstances of several familiar characters. One character, Prop Joe (Robert F. Chew), makes the final transition when he is murdered, while his killer, Marlo (Jamie Hector), ascends to replace him in the drug-dealing hierarchy. Another, a police officer named Carver (Seth Gilliam) who has recently moved up in rank, confronts the demands of new and heavier job requirements. Formerly willing to shirk responsibility, he now sees situations from "the other side of the desk" and becomes sensitized to the real-life consequences of not enforcing policies around community relations. When a hothead under his command loses it and attacks a schoolteacher in the midst of a routine drug bust, Carver refuses to "play along to get along." He reports the transgression to his superiors and weathers the officer's accusation that he is a rat. In an effort to get Carver to withdraw his complaint, the other officers enlist the help of Carver's former partner, Herc (Domenick Lombardozzi).

Carver and Herc meet in the precinct parking lot to share a beer and discuss the situation. I was looking forward to directing this scene precisely because of the ways it dramatizes the evolution of these two characters, whose misadventures have been a hallmark of previous seasons. The scene starts with Herc attempting to schmooze Carter, hoping to bring him back into the fold of the brotherhood of cops. Carver doesn't answer directly, but instead pointedly reminds Herc of a misstep we saw Herc make in the previous season that resulted in the downfall of Randy, one of the most endearing and aspirational youths to emerge from the brutal drug subculture. Herc attempts to slough it off in the manner we would expect from him. But Carver doesn't let him. "So what?" he asks. "So it mattered," Carver replies. "It all matters. I know we thought it didn't, but it does." Herc is meant to recognize the profound change in his former partner, who will no longer excuse irresponsible behavior — Herc's or his own. Chagrined, Herc abandons his mission and tells Carver to ignore the slights he is sure to get from his disgruntled troops because he is doing the right thing.

It's a powerful moment between two well-known characters that marks a seismic shift in their relationship. In directing the actors, I worked to physicalize the conflict, positioning the actors in view of Herc's new car, a Mercedes — symbolic of his corrupt new lifestyle working for a crooked lawyer. Carver turns to face Herc when he delivers the key lines so that Herc, already open and facing Carver in supplication, might experience the full force of the awful consequences for which he is responsible. The actors gave powerful, understated performances that perfectly realized a transition right before our eyes.

I knew those were the moments I wanted to deliver to the audience, but I also was aware that the power might be enhanced if I could somehow create a space, a context, that made the moment more significant. At some point during prep, I recalled a scene from an earlier season in which officers shared an after-hours beer in the precinct parking lot, then ritually hurled their empty cans and bottles onto the rooftop. It was treated as a throwaway scene (no pun intended), offering a glimpse into the lives and behaviors of the real Baltimore police, who actually did engage in that practice. David Simon, the show's creator, always loved to inject authentic touches like that into *The Wire*. This one had simply been a grace note, dropped into a much earlier episode and never referenced again. It occurred to me that an interesting introduction to the scene between Carver and Herc might be to start from the rooftop, with the camera skimming over hundreds of discarded cans and bottles to reveal the two men sharing a beer in the lot below. What this would create, I believed, was a sort of ritual space. It located the scene within a tradition of police officers letting their hair down with their brothers-in-arms and speaking to each other in a genuine, less inhibited way. To show a transition occurring in *that* space would suggest a deeper change occurring in the culture of policing itself. Creating the historical context might generate a more satisfying, richer viewing experience. It also changed the story into one that, I hoped, would have more significance.

Yet another way attention to context can serve storytelling is manipulation of point of view. Through which character's eyes are we seeing a scene? A sudden shift in perspective can open up the story in startling ways. In a season five episode of the show *House* entitled "Locked In," the story concerned a patient suffering from locked-in syndrome. This terrible affliction prevents a patient from moving any part of the body or making any sounds. The only outer marker that they are conscious at all is the flitting of the eyes, which can easily be mistaken for involuntary movement. The writers wanted Hugh Laurie's title character, Dr. House, to treat a patient with this ailment, which of course he does with his usual panache. The first half of the episode was told through the point of view of the patient himself, much like in *The Diving Bell and the Butterfly*, the feature film that inspired the episode. I employed the same specialty lens used in the film — called a Lensbaby — to put the audience in the patient's point of view, seeing only what he sees. The viewer feels privy to the patient's thoughts, which we hear, though he is powerless to speak. The lens creates dream-like imagery in which focus can be partially blurred, even within the same focal plane. Imagine, from the patient's perspective, seeing a face with only one eye in focus, then having that eye go blurry as the cheek or lip comes into sharp relief. Using this lens is a wonderful way of putting the viewer into what feels like the subjective state of a cognitively impaired man, locked away from communicating with the world.

At the end of the episode, once House has cured the patient, he engages in his customary banter with his colleague Wilson (Robert Sean Leonard). Throughout the episode, Wilson has been puzzled as to why House has avoided answering questions concerning where he's recently been. Wilson confronts House with the fact that he has figured out that House has actually gone to see a psychiatrist to help with his obvious psychological issues around intimacy, vulnerability, and drug dependency. Wilson says this as a friend, wanting to congratulate House on his courage in finally doing something about his debilitating depression. House responds by erasing the psychiatrist's contact information from his cell phone, then mockingly waving the phone at a mortified Wilson, who wants nothing more than for his friend to continue getting the help he needs. Walking away from Wilson and into an elevator, House is awash in pride and bravado. He proclaims that he is through seeking help because he doesn't need it. As the elevator doors close, Wilson cautions that House's stubbornness will condemn him to always being alone. It's a powerful warning and goes to the heart of House's overarching story in the series.

It struck me that this was an opportunity to use the camera lens we had established for the point of view of the character suffering from locked-in syndrome. I shot a close-up of Wilson from House's viewpoint using the Lensbaby. This shifted the sense of House's POV from a conventional one to that of someone perhaps screaming inside but unable to share their feelings. I asked Robert Sean Leonard to look directly into the lens, fuzzily in and out of focus, as he delivered his last line, "You'll be alone," with the elevator doors closing on House, sealed not only in the elevator but locked in a solitary confinement of his own making. The audience would be left with new insight that this character, who so entertains and fascinates us, is actually as much "locked-in" and suppressed as the patient we had seen suffer the excruciating illness. The story deepened and touched on something fundamental to the show's main character, making a connection that might otherwise have been missed.

I don't want to imply that a great deal of contextual information must be spoon-fed to viewers before they can enter our stories. We, as well as our audience, are products of our culture and already bring many assumptions and values that, in some sense, contextualize for us the programs we watch. But it's important to be careful how you define the world of your story in order to focus the audience's attention on the specific story you're telling. Poorly conceived or executed projects can ramble aimlessly between different expectations and ethical standards that their creators may not even be aware have been established. Not taking responsibility for the ground rules or contexts created in each moment can result in a loss of impact and credibility. Remember: Context results from the choices you make, approve, or ignore. Your story has a better chance of taking flight if you carefully monitor the world you want your audience to inhabit as they experience each moment you're charged with helping to create.

CHAPTER FOUR

MAKING MEANING: *HOMELAND*

I T'S RARE THAT I'LL READ A SCRIPT and feel immediately I know just how to tell the story. There are times new material excites me, and I can recognize its potential. But even then — maybe *especially* then — I'm aware of how much I don't yet know about how to direct it. Understanding only comes from delving into the material (usually with the assistance of the writers, actors, and crew) to discover insights I don't yet have.

I am frequently teased around my household that, when I first get a script, I tend to complain, "I got the worst one." Far more often than not, I've been mistaken — I just haven't yet done the work to understand the story and see its possibilities.

However you feel about the script you're given, though, you're going to be shooting it before very long. Your only choice is to do the best you can to bring it to life. Sometimes that will feel like a bigger challenge than at other times. When yours is a challenging script, the best you can hope for is that you're working on a good show with talented people. Such was the case when I was directing an episode for the seventh season of *Homeland*.

Homeland is a show I was privileged to work on for seven of its eight seasons. It was always an exciting assignment because of the quality of the writing, the topicality of the subject matter, and the extraordinary talent associated with it. The relationship between CIA agent Carrie Mathison (Claire Danes) and CIA senior official Saul Berenson (Mandy Patinkin) was one of the most nuanced, sophisticated, and beautifully acted in all of television. The show's storytelling kept viewers on the edge of their seats for the full duration of the series.

I had been fortunate in previous seasons to direct several of the show's significant episodes, including season four's "13 Hours in Islamabad," in which the American embassy in Pakistan is overrun by Muslim extremists. For a director, that was like winning the lottery, since the episode was filled with unimaginably high stakes, shocking action sequences, and heartbreaking loss. And as filming for season seven progressed, each new script kept me enthralled. The political dysfunction and dramatic tension built to excruciating levels through the first nine episodes. I couldn't wait to see how it would escalate in "mine," which was next up.

But the script I received essentially called a time-out on all the high-stakes international drama. Instead, it focused on a custody trial in which Carrie was being charged as an unfit parent for her four-year-old daughter, Franny. There were some additional storylines, but with Carrie preoccupied with her legal challenges, those felt to me a little like they were treading water, laying the groundwork for payoffs in later episodes. Carrie's battles with her sister about parenting Franny had occurred over several seasons, and to many viewers — myself included — they had begun to feel like the same story beat: Carrie would insist she was there for her daughter despite clearly being hugely distracted, while her sister, Maggie

(Amy Hargreaves), claimed otherwise. And now there would be a lengthy series of scenes, culminating in a fourteen-page trial, bringing this storyline to a close.

In addition, the courtroom scenes consisted only of a parade of witnesses testifying against Carrie's competence as a parent. We think of trial sequences as an aggressive confrontation of opposing views, with accusations leveled, evidence presented, and a spirited defense. But here there was no scripted cross-examination or even a single witness supportive of Carrie. There was only unchallenged testimony detailing her compromised performance as a parent, descriptions of events with which viewers of the show were already familiar. The trial would end with Carrie understanding that she really wasn't a fit parent for Franny and voluntarily relinquishing custody to her sister. One more element in the mix: Carrie had just undergone electroshock therapy and was deprived of her usual range of emotions.

To recap: My courtroom sequence, the episode's primary drama, was one-sided, all of the evidence had been heard or seen before, and our hero was emotionally dulled by thousands of volts of electricity to her brain. Plus, it ended with a whimper. Making this compelling was going to be a challenge.

But that was my job.

How to attack it? First, it's essential for a guest director to understand what the show's producers think an episode contributes to the overall arc of the series. In this case, the writers had reached a character climax of sorts, bringing Carrie to the tough epiphany that, to fulfill her destiny and continue to fight to save the world, she would have to make a major personal sacrifice. It exemplified the kind of attention to character that made *Homeland* the great show that it was, rich in human details informing its white-knuckled storylines. But here the domestic side of Carrie's character would be the central drama, and it would rehash material pretty well explored already.

The tone meeting gave me valuable insight into what I felt was the courtroom scene's problematic one-sidedness. The recent electroshock therapy stripped away Carrie's driven and defensive reactions, which had clouded her interactions with Maggie in the past. The reason the script offered no defense from Carrie was that the writers wanted the dramatic focus to be that she is hearing about her behavior as if for the first time and finally registers her sister's arguments. She is able to see, at last, that she is not the best parent for Franny. This would be a huge reckoning for her character.

This background perspective from the writers was helpful. But it still left me with a directing problem: how to create some surprise at the outcome of a lengthy, one-sided trial. The writers had their larger agenda, which was for Carrie to be freed from the burdens of parenting Franny in order to take the story where they intended for the remainder of the current and following seasons. But my job was to make this a compelling episode that could stand on its own.

In order to keep the viewers engaged, I felt it was important that they have some sense that Carrie has a chance to win the trial. The writers' point, that Carrie hears all the damning evidence and finally understands how wounding she has been to Franny, doesn't suggest much in the way of a fighting spirit to prevail. Nowhere is there even a peep from her attorney to rebut the witnesses. The script did have one dramatic device: Carrie has information that she could use to blackmail her sister, pressuring Maggie with career suicide if she refuses to withdraw her claim. But this carried its own storytelling challenge: It didn't give the audience much reason to root for our hero.

If the drama was to have any wind in its sails, I thought it essential that the audience believe Carrie is still committed to winning custody, right up to the moment she relents. That turn needed to be surprising and unexpected in order to deliver the dramatic impact basic storytelling requires. Otherwise, we might as well score the whole fourteen-page trial with a funeral dirge.

The best solution I could come up with was that, while Carrie comes to understand her parental failings, she ought at the same time to strongly believe that this new, clearer way she is now seeing herself will keep her from ever repeating her reckless behavior. In the process of the trial, the sense should be that she gains insight previously unavailable to her. Her instinctive strategy becomes to model this to the court by being contained, respectful, and absolutely committed to her daughter. Her unspoken message would be that no one could love Franny as much as she.

This called for an extraordinary performance from Claire Danes: There would be nothing available to her but silent emotions and facial reactions as she registers both the humility of accepting her own horrific behavior and the sadder but wiser conviction that she is still the right guardian for her child. I took some comfort in knowing that, if anybody could pull off such a challenging assignment, it was Claire.

I asked for a rare pre-production meeting with her to share my take on the material, interested in what her thoughts might be from the perspective of her intimacy with the character. I also knew that this was the sort of complicated, nuanced intention that would be unfair to spring on her the day of shooting. As always, she was thoughtful and acknowledged the difficulty of the challenge. She appreciated the competing needs within the storytelling: to justify Carrie relinquishing her own daughter and to maintain audience involvement in the outcome of the trial. It was important, despite all the damning testimony, that dramatic suspense be preserved until the final outcome, with the audience wondering, despite all the odds against her, how Carrie might still win. My approach made sense to Claire, who I knew could maneuver this tightrope impeccably. I still wished I could convince the writers to provide some cross-examination that might make clear Carrie was still putting up a fight, but that wasn't going to happen.

No matter how brilliant a performance might be counted on from Claire, I knew I could not rely on her alone to address all the challenges of making this sequence compelling. Her job was to be Carrie Mathison; mine was to be the storyteller, to give the experience shape and meaning. If I couldn't contextualize her performance by providing the audience with a way to understand her associations and transitions, the audience (and Claire) would be shortchanged.

If the courtroom sequence was the centerpiece of the episode, the centerpiece of the courtroom scenes was Maggie's testimony. It starts with Maggie delivering a tough attack on Carrie that evolves into a softer approach, with Maggie trying to let her sister know that this action is not personal but motivated only by concern for Franny. Maggie speaks of how much she admired Carrie when they were children and envied her special place within the family. Then, building on this opportunity to reach her sister, Maggie calls her a hero for all the sacrifices she has made in her service to the country.

The testimony ends with Carrie in great conflict about how she should respond. With the court in recess, and Maggie standing in the corridor with her lawyers and husband, Carrie suddenly rushes to her, clutching the "ticking time bomb": the blackmail material. The writers, of course, meant this to signal that Carrie might indeed deliver the low blow in order to prevail, but she does not; instead, she tells her sister that she will allow Franny to go with her.

With all of the devastating testimony against Carrie, with Maggie piling on, and with Claire having to convey that Carrie understands what an awful mother she's been, I struggled with how to avoid making the ending predictable and anticlimactic. In particular, I worried about where the key moment might be when the audience could experience — really feel *with* Claire — the momentous turn. The writers had told me it should be when Maggie calls her a hero. But I kept wondering why Carrie would take her at her word. After all the attacks, why would it not feel simply like a bone Maggie was throwing her in order to assuage her guilt for taking away the person Carrie loves most in the world? It's easy to say nice things when you know you're going to get what you want.

A fourteen-page sequence takes considerable time to shoot, easily more than a day. We'd shot a good deal of the witness testimony on day one and were scheduled to put Maggie on the stand the following day. Claire had done an excellent job, as she listened to the parade of incriminating social workers and school principals, of conveying the sense of becoming increasingly self-aware at the same time that she was certain this experience would make her a better parent. The next day's testimony from Maggie would have to reverse that certainty.

In a story, you can *want* specific things to happen, you can *say* that they happen, and you can do your best to justify *why* they happen. But that's not the same as creating the *feeling* that they, credibly, have happened. Bad drama is filled with false moments in which characters go through transformations that have not been earned, with false insights and false feelings ramrodding the story along. In some ways, this is how melodrama works — maybe even what defines melodrama: We get to see what we want without experiencing the authentic way real human beings react in real situations. How do we know what real authenticity looks and feels like? By testing it against what we know about people, about life, and about what moves us; by checking to see if it's something we instinctively find credible.

Something felt false to me about the whole setup meant to dramatize Carrie's momentous turn. I knew what the writers wanted to have happen and how they thought it should be understood: that Carrie is moved when Maggie calls her a hero, and this somehow frees her to relinquish Franny. I didn't buy it. In my mind, it left too much unresolved in the bitter relationship between the two sisters. I thought it more likely that Carrie would respond to Maggie's praise by being wary and dismissive, not wanting to be played by a compliment. Of course, I could ask Claire to *play* that she is deeply moved, but I didn't feel this reaction would be earned. I felt it would be manipulative, there simply to bring about a desired outcome.

Moments of reckoning that have moved me — either in life or in great storytelling — have taught me that transformation has a chance to occur when people honestly confront something about themselves that they've been unaware of or strenuously denying. When they give up their own failed strategies or self-deceptions, it can feel like a death. Transformation starts with being willing to admit to painful truths, which can break through our fixed ideas about ourselves and our defenses keeping them intact. The possibility arises for grace to appear, giving us a fuller awareness of, and forgiveness for, who we really are. Dramatizing this, to me, is the height of great storytelling, and transformation is probably the most personally meaningful theme I am drawn to explore in any story. For this *Homeland* episode, the writers demonstrated a similar understanding in how they described Carrie's journey: She finally sees how unfit she's been as a parent, and this painful reckoning leads her to do the right thing for her daughter. But it was not landing for me, nor would it, I imagined, for the audience. In thinking about Maggie's testimony for the following day, I kept asking myself how the momentousness of Carrie's shift in perspective might be credibly rendered: What would it take to move me if I were in Carrie's place?

What came to me with a flash of illumination was that perhaps I had been too preoccupied with Carrie's inner reckoning. Maybe the key was in Maggie's.

It was easy to think of Carrie as the focal point of the drama (she was) and to lose sight of the fact that what was being dramatized was not simply a custody battle, but the rapprochement between two sisters who have a troubled history. Throughout the series, Maggie often stood in judgment of Carrie for her irresponsible behavior. Even when she had helped out with Franny, things never felt easy between the two. Now they both have entered this fray, and each is determined to win at any cost.

There are all sorts of ways for an actor to play a scene plausibly and naturally. But the most important question to answer is:

What intention would give the moment its due? Maggie's testimony included some spontaneous remarks that departed from her prepared notes and addressed Carrie directly. Up to this point, I had understood this part of her testimony in the same way it was discussed in the tone meeting: Maggie's intention is to give Carrie a simpler, more down-to-earth explanation — free of acrimony and posturing — of how they'd gotten to this place. She means Carrie no harm and, in fact, has always regarded her as a hero. But she, Maggie, would be the better parent for Franny. This was intended to bring Carrie around, but I felt it wasn't enough to justify her turn.

I sensed there might be another way to consider Maggie's intention so as to accomplish everything I and the writers wanted. What if the resolution involved Maggie having to pay almost as big a price as Carrie? What if, in her testimony, she has to own up to something she has resisted admitting her entire life because it was too painful and made her feel terribly deficient? What if we, and Carrie, could watch Maggie experience this awareness, which she owns up to as she makes her confession?

In her spontaneous words, Maggie tells Carrie that she has always felt inferior to her, less admired by their father and less daring. Might it be that she mentions this in her testimony not just to de-escalate the acrimony in the proceedings but to accomplish something more crucial? To come clean in this public setting — at great personal cost — about what she has never before admitted to Carrie. Her secret could be that she still battles feelings of envy and inadequacy, and these feelings have been responsible for some of her angry behavior toward her sister. Certainly, Carrie's mood swings and obsessive behavior have lent credibility to Maggie's concerns for Franny. But Maggie may also have used them as cover, wanting always to appear to be taking the high road, to be the reasonable and responsible one, when in truth (or the truth I wanted to convey) her actions were always tinged with a little sanctimoniousness and passive aggression.

I felt it was important to make Maggie's true feelings about her sister, which she discloses in her testimony, a secret that still wounds her. Admitting to it in this public and official setting might be the most difficult thing she has ever had to do. This would give the actress something extraordinary to play, as well as meet the conditions for meaningful transformation to occur: first Maggie's, and then, because of it, Carrie's. Why might she be compelled to bare her soul precisely now? Because she is about to take from Carrie the person her sister most loves in life, causing pain from which she might never recover. It almost certainly is the last time Carrie will ever give Maggie an opportunity to be heard. The unfinished business between them, namely Maggie's unacknowledged resentment and jealousy, has festered throughout her entire life. In the future, if Carrie were to learn of this resentment in another context, it would cast this custody battle in an abhorrent light, leading Carrie to the suspicion that it had not been for the child's well-being, but was a mean and sadistic impulse of Maggie's to get back at the sister she resented. But this is *not* what motivates Maggie; it's her best self spurring her to protect Franny. To engage in what has become essentially a hostile takeover, she must be "clean" and know within herself that hostility is not what drives her. It's concern for a little girl. She must cleanse herself of her own mixed motives, thus depriving Carrie of a reason — even in some imagined future — to feel victimized because Maggie's motives had been impure.

After this revelation, I was faced with another case of not wanting to spring on an actor such a significant adjustment to her character's inner life moments before cameras were to roll. I called Amy Hargreaves, who played Maggie, and gave her this new way of imagining her testimony, which would be filmed the next afternoon. It was far more demanding than what she had been working with, but, like all good actors, Amy was excited to be challenged to go deeper. She delivered a masterful performance, mostly in subtext because the script did not linger on the sisters' history. But we could feel the price she was paying and could see her character's deeper humanity and new credibility. Claire, playing Carrie, registered it as well.

Now, I felt, we had finally arrived at a place where I could believe Carrie would be moved by Maggie calling her a hero. She would feel that the praise was untainted by any agenda, and it might help her feel less guilty about the demands of the career she had chosen. But the kicker, and the real reason to me she relents, is that she can now consider Maggie's words that *follow* this praise to be truthful. The sisters have met one another on a profound level, and Carrie has become more open to considering what her sister has to say. After Maggie compliments her, she goes on to point out that the historical record proves pretty conclusively that, once duty calls, Carrie will be unable to maintain her commitment to Franny. Carrie indeed has a noble calling, which drives her in ways even her conscious intentions cannot control, so isn't it inevitable Franny will suffer? *That* was the insight Carrie could finally take in for the first time.

The pieces were now in place for me to believe Carrie's decision to stand down. And I felt that the audience would believe it, too. The moment she approaches Maggie with the blackmail material provides a jolt of fear that perhaps Carrie is giving in to baser impulses. But the fact that she does not do so feels justified by the events we've just witnessed. I was very happy, also, that this new subtext had the added benefit of reimagining the entire history of the two sisters, lending depth and poignance to this family's journey.

I don't believe that this interpretation contradicted anything the writers had intended, and I was reminded how remarkable this collaborative process is, in which each of us contributes our unique perspectives and talents to the finished product. My job was to interpret the script and to present events in a way that ensured the most satisfying story experience. It was not the writers' job to tell me how to do that, nor to have to point out to me all the deeper intentions required to bring it about. Similarly, actors often will do their own inner work to bring added dimension to their characters, giving the story meaning it might not otherwise have. But it's the director who finally determines how the story is told and when it's the best version it can be.

I was struck, also, by how my insights grew organically from what the writers had provided me. Even my new way of imagining Maggie's speech was inspired by clues planted in the dialogue itself. I don't think the writers had identified the subtext I gave it, but I do believe that in the genesis of any project, writers, like other artists, draw upon their subconscious instincts. What may elude their conscious awareness is there for other collaborators to sense and develop through their own intuitive powers and artistry. The fact that no changes in the dialogue were required to accommodate the new intention leads me to believe that the writers were in touch at some level with the possibility for this interpretation to arise. Creativity involves working at deeper levels than just conscious awareness, and the beauty of this collaborative art is that it invites humility and openness to what others may contribute.

This episode, entitled *Clarity*, may have disappointed a segment of the fan base that tuned in primarily for the show's mix of political intrigue, espionage, and mortal peril. I imagine, too, that the subtle levels of intention I worked so hard to sharpen may have eluded some viewers' conscious awareness. But the episode was deeply satisfying to me because it took the character dynamics to a meaningful place. What compels one director about a piece of material might not interest another. What bothers one — as I was bothered by what felt to me like unmotivated behavior — slides easily off the back of another. We each bring our own instincts and style to the job. Those are the things on which you have to rely. I felt that a moment that had to happen hadn't been earned, and I asked a series of questions that led me to a solution that felt right. But I don't think that would have happened if I hadn't stayed committed to satisfying myself that the story had finally yielded its deeper truths. That commitment is what gives you the best chance to enrich the meaning and the life of the story you're telling.

CHAPTER FIVE

WHAT STORY ARE YOU TELLING?

T HE ROLE OF THE DIRECTOR ON AN episode of television is storyteller. While the script is, of course, a constant touch-stone, it has to be interpreted. That is the director's job. It's true that in taking the reins of an episode it's the showrunner's vision you serve; they will doubtless have specific ideas about how the story works. But in many senses, the script is a fleshless blueprint. There is no such thing as simply "filming the script." That would be pictures of words on a page.

An audience's experience of an episode comes from a wide variety of elements, not simply the story as written in the script. It's the result of all the ways you have chosen to present the material, including, among many other things, the performances you're able to draw from your actors, blocking and integrating those performances with one another, the camera work you supervise, and all the contributions from the various departments that seek your input and approval. It's your responsibility to advance the story moment by moment, focusing viewers' attention exactly where you want it to maintain engagement.

With all that responsibility, how is one to know the right thing to do?

If you aren't connected to a vision of the story you're telling — and, just as importantly, if you aren't connected by *caring* about it — you will have a much harder time trusting yourself with each creative decision. You certainly won't always know with certainty that a given choice is the right one. But being emotionally invested in your story will strengthen your intuition and the chance of getting it right.

That can be more complicated than most people think. A story is more than simply what happens; it includes the *meaning* of what happens. Your job as director is to point the audience to what is significant, fleshing out the characters and enriching the story on levels you have great power to influence. The director's efforts in those areas account for why one "love story," for example, lands more deeply for an audience than another.

You shouldn't be shy about asking the writer or showrunner about anything for which you need more clarity. Chances are they have thought more deeply than you about how the story works and what it's about at the less obvious levels of character and meaning. But ultimately, it matters less how connected they are to the story than that you find your own connection to it. Perhaps it will exactly mirror theirs, but it has to become your own. You cannot tell a story well if you do not own it. By caring about what gets communicated and, better still, by staying curious yourself about the questions and issues the story raises, you have a greater chance of capturing your audience's imagination.

Storytelling itself is as old as the human species. Stories are revered in every culture. People have huddled around fires to hear tales and gathered to watch dramas for longer than recorded history because there is a hunger for stories deep within our psyches. Stories are fundamental to the meaning we ascribe to the world and to who we take ourselves to be. We are so driven by narrative and the need for coherence in our lives that most people would rather live out a bad story than face the void of having no story at all.

All of us live in a story. Some of us are aware of the stories we tell ourselves and are aware that they are stories. Others assume their story is reality. We develop a narrative about our lives, usually based on past experience, and cling to it even if it defines us as deficient, rejected, or needing to be rescued by someone else. Some are fortunate to have empowering stories that define them as capable and ready for a challenge. But regardless of a story's merits, we inhabit them to feel secure in knowing who we are, or to think we know who we are, even if that story leads to pain and suffering for ourselves or for others. Among the most powerful ways to affect people is to invite them to reconsider the stories with which they've identified.

There is an incredible moment in the film *Witness* (directed by Peter Weir) that illustrates this fact beautifully. The story centers on an Amish community and its refusal to engage in physical violence. Throughout the movie, Amish characters hold to their cherished value of turning the other cheek. The patriarch of the heroine's family maintains that, even when it seems physical retaliation is the only way to deal with an attack, there is always another way. Harrison Ford, playing hard-nosed and pugnacious Philadelphia cop John Book, convalesces in the community. He is recovering from gunshot wounds he suffered while protecting a young Amish boy, witness to a crime. The community elders, as well as the child's mother, Rachel (Kelly McGillis), insist that Book surrender his handgun while he is living with them. When the dirty police officers behind the crime show up to kill both Book and the boy, Rachel and her father are held at gunpoint so Book will surrender. The patriarch sees the child witness hiding just out of sight of the captors and makes a gesture to the boy, opening and closing his fist.

I think most viewers assumed, as I did, that the patriarch is signaling the only action that made sense: "Go get the handgun; it's our only option." As the scene unfolds and the dirty cops parade Book toward the police car, the community bell begins to clang loudly. This was what the elder was indicating for the young boy to do: grab hold of the rope of the community bell and ring it. The entire town converges on the square, confronting the cops with the impossible choice of having to kill everyone if they want to take John Book. I was startled to recognize my own unconscious bias that only violence could solve certain problems; I had superimposed that assumption onto the story being told. The elder believed in and lived by a different narrative, one that was more humane. The audience was able to absorb the wisdom of it at the same time that they were made aware of their own unquestioned assumptions, their different story. Novelist Richard Powers has said, "The best arguments in the world won't change a person's mind. The only thing that can do that is a good story."

As directors, it's important to know the stories we struggle with inside ourselves. Unless we identify them, we may bring them to bear on tales that want to go in different directions. We might force one of our own narratives onto the story we're supposed to be telling. If we, consciously or unconsciously, hold on to personal stories at odds with the material, we're likely to cut ourselves off from greater possibilities.

Playwright and screenwriter Robert Anderson wrote a wrenching play about a father-son relationship entitled *I Never Sang for My Father*. I don't believe the movie adaptation did it justice, but the stage version is very powerful. The play concerns the relationship between a dutiful, middle-aged son and his charismatic but overbearing father. The father was once a dominant figure in the world but now, in old age, is unable to accept his declining powers. The self-absorbed and narcissistic father has emasculated his son through incessant demands that have forced the younger man to sacrifice his own ambitions. The son was never able to stand up to his father for fear of offending, wounding, or provoking the man he idealized and admired. The climax of the play involves the son at last confronting his father.

In a post-performance question-and-answer session with the playwright, Anderson was asked to describe the writing process of the devastating final encounter. He told how this was very much his own story and that he, like the protagonist, was paralyzed when it came to claiming his own life if it meant disappointing or hurting his father. When trying to write the scene, he repeatedly came up against a brick wall because he had, in fact, never confronted his dad. He recognized that his imagination was stuck in the dependent role he was playing in his own life. He concluded that the only way to write something true to what the story required was to have that encounter with his real-life father. He found the strength to do so and transcribed the exchange almost verbatim, creating a tremendously powerful theatrical experience, full of catharsis and self-realization. Because of a commitment to pursue the story he had set into motion wherever it led, he was able to overcome a lifetime of fear and self-protection. For Anderson to have his creative breakthrough, he had to become consciously aware of the personal story he was living out, which depended on the belief that he would be undone if he ever confronted his father. Seeing how this inner narrative was compromising his artistic effort empowered him to choose to serve the story he was writing and to find the courage to challenge the self-limiting story of his own life.

How, as directors, does this apply to us? Like writers, we are inventing a story with every choice we make by focusing the audience's attention on what is at stake. If our personal narratives are at odds with the story that wants to be told, we might not tell that story in a way for the audience to fully experience it; we might not, for example, help an actor find the appropriate subtext for their character's dialogue. If an actor's lines are spoken without awareness of what is at issue, they simply won't be understood in the way the writer intended. Or we might be satisfied with moments that don't land in a way that points the characters (and the audience) to the understanding we may be avoiding, protecting ourselves by not venturing into emotional areas that are personally unsettling.

We will find better, more honest solutions to the storytelling challenges we face if we truly know our own narratives. Then we can choose either to make use of the insights they offer or, if they do not apply, set them aside. What really makes for exciting storytelling is when we bring an adventurousness to the process and open ourselves to making discoveries based on what the material calls forth from us. If we are not willing to be challenged, we probably won't have much to say.

Always ask yourself as you read a script, or watch a scene unfold in rehearsal, or even after take seven: What is the story I am following? Is it a story worthy of my attention? If not, what might make it so? Once you ask yourself this, your imagination will be activated to seek and provide an answer. If you aren't engaged in trying to make the story better, you aren't likely to be happy with the results. And you're depriving all of us — your actors, writers, employers, and viewers — of what you alone can bring to this job, what you uniquely see through the lens of your own imagination. Your job is, first and foremost, to serve the story. But how you steer the audience in that pursuit is more within your power than you might imagine, as is defining the meaning of the story.

One of my favorite shows of the '90s is *Northern Exposure,* a comedy that I think ranks right up there with any in our so-called "golden age." It followed the lives of the wildly eccentric townspeople in a remote community, the fictitious Cicely, Alaska. The creators of the show, Joshua Brand and John Falsey, once described its focus as being "confrontation with 'the other.'" How do unique, fiercely independent, peculiar characters get along with one another when each one of them seems bizarrely idiosyncratic? Most have come to Cicely out of a desire to flee civilization and live by their own rules rather than conform to somebody else's. The show took advantage of its unconventional characters by unveiling all manner of spiritual or esoteric possibilities in a part tongue-in-cheek, part sincere exploration of existential and philosophic questions. It was a great "fish out of water" story, featuring for its first five seasons the attempts of a young Jewish doctor from New York City (Rob Morrow) to fit in as he fulfills his contract to provide medical services to Cicely, which had underwritten his medical school tuition. I felt thrilled and privileged to direct several episodes over the show's last three seasons and was sorry to have to say goodbye when I completed work on what I thought would be my last opportunity. Because of declining ratings, it was clear that the show would not be renewed for a seventh season. Rob Morrow had left to pursue a feature-film career and, in my view, CBS never really gave *Northern* a strong chance to recover from

Rob's departure, moving it to a new time slot without publicizing the change. In those ancient days of the 1990s, you had to actually watch a show the night it aired, or miss it entirely and never be counted as a viewer. The writing was on the wall.

I got a call a few weeks after I'd left, however, asking if I might be free on short notice to fly back to Seattle, where *Northern Exposure* filmed, and direct one more episode. I was told that the director had dropped out over creative differences. I also soon learned that he was not alone in feeling angered by the script, which several cast members felt had jumped the shark, meaning that it betrayed their characters' credibility simply to produce an unearned comedic effect. Because the showrunner (David Chase, who would later go on to create *The Sopranos*) and the episode's writing team (Robin Green and Mitchell Burgess) knew I would be walking into a bit of a maelstrom, they told me what I would be up against if I accepted the job. I asked to read the script.

The story concerned the efforts of the wife of the new doctor in town, another fish out of water from New York City, to ingratiate herself to her new community by directing a local theater production of William Inge's play *Bus Stop*. The wife, Michelle (Teri Polo), is introduced in the episode as she asks the town's resident gay couple for a financial contribution to support the production. Ron (Doug Ballard) writes an extravagantly large check so that Michelle will cast his partner, Erick (Don McManus), on the condition that she never reveal the financial incentive that led her to cast him. Erick had years ago abandoned his hopeless acting career, and Ron now simply wants to perk him up. This starts Michelle on a journey for which she did not realize she was signing up: a descent into chaos. In the unfolding of the story, the script portrayed the disintegration of the community. Suddenly, characters viewers had known for years begin transforming into bizarro-world clones of themselves. They struggle with inner demons, the theater's toll for unleashing the free play of their imaginations, which strips them bare of their defenses. Those defenses are revealed to have protected them from confronting what most terrifies and embarrasses them: their secret weaknesses and deficiencies.

I loved the script.

I had a completely different take on the story from the first director and from those cast members who felt they were being asked to betray the integrity of their characters. The town's restaurant proprietor, Holling Vincoeur (Broadway great John Cullum), reacts to his stage fright by drinking excessively. The coolest of cool deejays, Chris Stevens (John Corbett, later to star in *Sex in the City* and *My Big Fat Greek Wedding*), is paralyzed by fear at the prospect of kissing his co-lead, Maggie O'Connell (Janine Turner). The town hottie, Shelly Tambo (Cynthia Geary), is reduced to sputtering insecurity as she fails to get cast as the romantic lead. Erick, the failed actor, becomes so narcissistically inflated that he lapses into obnoxious pretentiousness and overbearing self-importance, only to collapse in near suicidal despair when he learns the truth of why he'd been cast. And all the town's tradespeople throw themselves into stagehand work with a fervor bordering on mania. When things deteriorate seemingly beyond repair, the men retreat to a backwoods still, crying into their beers and wallowing in abject self-pity. Then, somehow, the show goes on and, magically, order is restored to the community.

I understood why people felt so thrown by the script. It was true, cast members were being asked to play intentions and phobias they'd never before dreamed their characters were capable of. I sympathized with their bruised feelings and respected the integrity they were trying to uphold. But I felt strongly that they had missed what the story was, and that if they approached it with a different understanding — which was my job to convey to them — they would embrace it as a beautiful example of *Northern*'s bold and adventurous sensibility.

What the story was about, it seemed to me, was the thin veneer we each construct to present ourselves to the world. This conceals, not just from others, but from ourselves, our own disappointing truths: the longings and deficiencies we are afraid to admit and the vulnerability that can be triggered when we lose the security of our familiar social roles. Theater invites the full play of our imagination, the relinquishing of "what we know" (or want to believe) in favor of what might arise spontaneously from within. That is what, at times, human beings most fear. This is particularly true for characters who have fled previous circumstances precisely not to have to face uncomfortable realities. It was a comic revelation that the characters in *Northern Exposure*, who seemed so refreshingly authentic, were, like most of us, running from facing their deepest vulnerabilities. The story seemed to imply that social contracts are simply agreements whereby we support each other in our own self-deceptions, and that if we were really to face the truth of our natures, we might not like what we see. This particular story contained an optimistic truth: that what we most fear confronting can lead to a more integrated and self-accepting experience of ourselves.

Comedy (and, in a different way, drama as well) is often about the revelation of a truth that has been masked by some kind of taboo. Laughter erupts from the shock of recognizing something we may have known but have kept secret from our conscious awareness. It could therefore be totally within character for Holling to be harboring desperate stage fright, something he'd never before had to confront; or for Chris never to have acknowledged to himself his romantic attraction to Maggie for fear of being rejected and no longer appearing quite so cool; or for Shelly to be thrown by the loss of a social role on which she depended for self-esteem; or for Erick to be caught up in unresolved narcissism that he reexperiences because of his partner's well-intentioned meddling. All of this chaos is precipitated and framed by the magic of the theater. What emerges is a newly imagined, more inclusive community. In keeping with the broader themes of the series, the episode dramatizes a confrontation with "the other." Only, in this instance, it was the *other* within *ourselves*: those unacknowledged impulses and identities the characters are so threatened by.

I had great fun directing this episode, entitled "Buss Stop," a fanciful wordplay on the play's title and on the romantic kiss Chris is finally able to give Maggie. The actors, with only the slightest of prompts from me, grew to sense the real story we were telling and gave themselves to all of the character foibles humorously explored in each scene. It turned out to be one of my favorite episodes of *Northern*, despite the warnings that came with the assignment. It did not need a rewrite but simply a redefinition of the story, which illustrates the power you have as the director. I actually thought it was a brilliant script and didn't have to work too hard to find what interested me in it. But however much we feel our insights flow directly from the script, our take on the material is deeply influenced by our natures, our interests, and our imaginations. They can point us to the story that is ours to tell. On the director's journey, that's really all we have to offer.

CHAPTER SIX

GETTING THE PERFORMANCE

WATCHING A GREAT PERFORMANCE TAKE SHAPE IS one of the true thrills of directing. Something emerges that is deep and revealing about being human. Helping your cast get there is among the director's most important responsibilities. Some projects are more actor dependent than others. But, in my experience, a story's impact is directly related to how much truthfulness, emotional honesty, and depth of understanding the actors bring to their performance. That's not to say that every *character* is truthful, honest, or deep. Quite the contrary. But actors who have accessed those qualities in *themselves* are in a better position to enrich the story.

Some actors require more help than others to break through emotional barriers or to develop a deeper understanding of their roles. The director's job is to provide that help. Many directors seem frightened of actors, or treat them as a different species. The clichés describing actors can run the gamut from narcissistic and self-absorbed to moody, vain, and temperamental. Of course, they can be any of those things. Just like directors. But stereotyping actors is usually the product of a director's own lack of familiarity with the acting process.

The best training I ever received as a director was the three years I studied to be an actor. In my twenties, I felt bottled up emotionally and looked at acting as a way of exploring new ways of being. It was exhilarating, and yet at times it put me squarely up against all the areas in my life where I was afraid, repressed, or hiding out. Acting class provided tools and opportunities to work through those barriers, to "get present" to one's fellow performers and to the imaginary circumstances of the dramatic material. Most people spend a lifetime relying on defenses to protect themselves from emotional pain. But actors are asked to actively court whatever arises as they explore the deeper truths of their characters.

It felt wonderful when I broke through, but too often in my performances, I felt mired in self-consciousness. It became clear that directing was my calling because as the director I was more able to get out of my own way. But what I received from my acting experience was a deep appreciation for actors, empathy for the challenges they face, and respect for their craft. An additional gift turned out to be all the techniques I had to develop in trying to arrive at a passable performance. These have helped me in assisting "real actors" to reach their own depths.

This is why I think it's a good idea for young directors to take at least one acting class themselves. Once you're asked to inhabit another character — to leave your own inner life and enter another's — you begin to discover some of the actor's challenges. Most of us have emotional constraints or tightly held images of ourselves that prevent full access to our feelings. In challenging yourself to work through those barriers, you begin to develop a sense of how an actor might be supported by the director.

Actors are just people, susceptible to the same foibles all of us experience. Their art requires courage, for they are often asked to explore emotions and behaviors outside of their comfort zones. When we watch a performance, we hope to see what it might be like to go through an experience we would rather never have or one that we can enjoy vicariously. In either instance, the goal should be for the actors to arrive at appropriate behavior in which they have fully invested as much depth of understanding and honesty as possible.

TRUST

Communicating with actors is an intimate process. Often you will be asking them to take emotional risks. And it's their skin in the game, not yours. An actor's inappropriate response or behavioral choice could be humiliating, even career damaging. If the actors don't trust you, imagine how much more difficult it makes their job. And yours. There really is no formula for developing trust. Each actor is a unique individual, and you'll need to rely on your own instincts when you determine how to relate to any actor. But there are a few things I think are crucial.

First, it's important to be as authentic as possible. This is a good goal generally because unless you can be ruthlessly honest with yourself, you probably won't be much of a director. When dealing with actors, however, authenticity is especially important since you want to be invited into their process. You want to contribute a sense of support and encouragement, which will only be meaningful if the actor believes you.

It's easy to be honest when the actor gives you exactly what you want and you have only nice things to say. Don't forget to demonstrate appreciation when that occurs; we all feel better when the good work we've done is acknowledged and valued. The more an actor feels supported and seen, the more likely they will be willing to go further in their explorations.

It becomes challenging when you have a difficult note to give. You may need to ask an actor to consider the scene in a vastly different way from their instincts. If you can't face their disappointment when you don't approve of their choice — and couch your note too obliquely, or misrepresent your true feelings — you run the risk of losing credibility or being misunderstood and perhaps not getting the performance you want. More importantly, you will have demonstrated a lack of respect for the actor's ability to hear the truth as you see it, to take your note, and possibly to build upon it in ways you might never have imagined.

I once worked with a very famous actor whom I greatly admired. I'll call him Max. He had created a number of memorable roles on both stage and screen, and was playing a part right in his wheelhouse: a charismatic, fierce leader of renegades, a character both brilliant and vicious. I was looking forward to what he would bring to the part and the exciting chance to work with him. In prep, I had introduced myself to begin the relationship, but this actor presented me with so reserved a demeanor that I couldn't shake the feeling of being coldly assessed. This had the effect of making me uncomfortably self-conscious, second-guessing everything I said to him. Our first day on set, we rehearsed a scene I couldn't wait to see him play. It started with Max's character approaching an underling to check on the repair of some broken machinery, crucial to Max's grand scheme; the other character was sickly and overwhelmed by the nearly impossible challenge. After watching rehearsal, I was shocked by how tepid and undramatic Max's choices had been. Not yet knowing his process or whether he was saving his performance for when filming began, I resisted giving him a note. But after the first take of the master angle, I saw that this was exactly how he had chosen to play it. I was stunned. Max was a world-class actor, yet this performance did nothing to advance the story, nor deepen the character. Worse, it was boring.

Max has one of the most intimidating presences I have ever encountered. He is famous for roles in which his fits of rage have left behind only scorched earth. His performances have opened up new vistas of thought and insight for me. To approach him on our first scene together to "correct" his choice was something that gave me great pause. Yet I knew I could not let this stand. I thought hard how to deliver a note that would not be insulting, that might spark in him the life that was missing.

In the scene, Max's character enters to check on the progress of his subordinate's work, only to learn that the man cannot guarantee the broken machinery can be repaired. Max then rehashes their history; how, when they first met, he considered the other man an entitled aristocrat who looked down on people like Max, rough-hewn men who were self-made, having risen from the lower classes and willing to do anything to get ahead. The man came to join Max because he had to flee from his own run-ins with authority, and there was mutual self-interest in making the relationship work. Now that many years have passed, and he has made a home under Max's stewardship, Max expresses the hope that the man will extend himself and make a concerted effort to somehow find a way to repair the broken device.

Max played the scene in a straightforward manner, rather docilely. His intentions seemed simple and supportive. He had taken the surface level of the dialogue literally, as if its gentility reflected his own inner state. For my money, he had lost the character's deviousness and fierce drive to accomplish his criminal scheme, which depended on the machine getting fixed. I approached Max and said, "I wonder if you might try something a little different. The contempt you describe having felt for him when you first met ... please try entering the scene still feeling exactly the same way." He answered simply, "Very well," though I couldn't be sure how he felt about my note.

On the next take, there was an immediate charge in the room as soon as he entered. He evinced an eerie calm, toying with the other man as he inquired into his progress. When he learned he was to be disappointed, Max began to spin the tale of their history, with a sinister undercurrent of threat that was chilling. The message was clear: Though the man had been given safe haven for many years, and his usefulness had made him acceptable, he was still, in Max's estimation, the same entitled aristocrat who had been tolerated only out of mutual self-interest. If his usefulness were to disappear by failing to provide needed services, so would his safety. Max exited, leaving the man newly desperate to solve the mystery of the broken device. What had been tepid and stale was now electric and terrifying. I was thrilled, marveling at how a great actor could take a suggestion and discover inner treasures that make a scene come to life. But I had no idea how Max felt about our interaction.

Days later, I was doing my laundry at the company's wardrobe trailer when the head costumer approached to say she had discussed me with Max. I went on alert, half expecting he'd resented my presumptuousness in questioning his choice. "He said he loves working with you. You're the first director to give him a note." I honestly had had no inkling that he'd approved either of me or the adjustment I'd given him. But the experience showed me how other directors likely had buckled under the fear of incurring the wrath of this formidable presence. Great actors like Max might rarely need adjusting, but sometimes they do. And if you can't figure out a way to provide it, your project will suffer. You will have compromised your own story instincts and risked losing your actors' trust that you will give them an honest response to their work.

SHARING THE STORY

The impact of a performance is influenced by how the director has framed it for the audience. The art of telling the story involves sensitizing the viewers to what is at stake, as well as bringing them to the precise subjective state needed to be most affected by a performance or by unfolding events. The actors themselves needn't be aware of every aspect of the storytelling, but, in my experience, a better performance is likely to result when the director has invited the actor to connect their exploration to the specific issues the story is investigating. Actors can benefit when directors share their point of view about what is at issue dramatically.

This is also an opportunity for the director to demonstrate command of the story, which can assist in building trust with actors. It's difficult enough for them to develop their own characterizations; to add worry about how their performance will fit into the overall narrative can be a distraction and undermine their confidence. Know your story and what compels you about it. The more you can create context for your actors and share your vision of where a particular moment fits, the easier it will be for them to settle into their own process. You might get discussion, even argument, about suggested adjustments. But I have found that it's effective to rely on story to help an actor shape their performance, particularly when you want to move an actor off a choice you feel is inappropriate.

In the fourth season of *Homeland*, I directed one of the most exciting scripts I have ever been handed. "13 Hours in Islamabad," written by Alex Gansa and Howard Gordon, dramatized the overthrow of the United States embassy in Pakistan. It brought together several storylines and character arcs that converged in a clash of outcomes that were tragic and wrenching. In one six-page sequence, Saul (Mandy Patinkin) is being debriefed on his period of captivity with Taliban terrorists by Peter Quinn (Rupert Friend), who is desperate to come up with a lead on their where-abouts. Thirty-seven Americans have been killed, and the Taliban leader, Haqqani (Numan Acar), has stolen a list of American "assets," each of whom is now likely to be "neutralized" and thus rendered unable to provide further critical intelligence. Carrie (Claire Danes) watches the debriefing but interrupts to call a halt to Quinn's aggressive tactics.

In the story, this sequence takes place the very night of the terrorist attack, just hours after unimaginable loss and defeat. Each character is dealing with their own brand of shell shock. Quinn witnessed the execution of several colleagues and narrowly missed capturing the fleeing Haqqani. Carrie had been pinned down in a brutal assault on her motorcade, an attack that killed several close associates and nearly herself as well. Also, just moments before Saul's interrogation, she learned that the President has lost faith in her, insisting she return home. And Saul, who was also pinned down in the motorcade with Carrie, is now tormented by the knowledge that his own lack of attentiveness most likely led to his capture, creating the conditions exploited by the Taliban to successfully overrun the American embassy.

All three of the characters in the scene, therefore, were undergoing their own personal crises. In addition, each needed to combine forces with the other two to develop an effective strategic plan. There was so much to be untangled that I asked for an hour before call time to fully rehearse the sequence, without the crew having to sit idly by (and on the clock) while we worked things out. I knew that with such consummate actors, we would arrive at something quite powerful, but I wanted to allow for a full exploration of all the nuances implicit in the material.

As I like to do when rehearsing complicated sequences, I started by restating the scene's historical antecedents to remind the cast of how their characters arrived at this precise moment, reacquainting them with story points they may have forgotten that ought to influence their choices. We read through the lines, then got the scene "on its feet" for the actors to find staging that felt appropriate. Rupert paced the tiny secure room as Mandy sat, head in hands, at the table. Claire was scripted to be positioned outside the glass-walled debriefing room, able to observe but not hear the goings-on inside. Rupert, as Quinn, projected an impatient and electric energy as he pressed Saul to try harder to come up with something, anything, he might recall from his captivity that could offer a lead to the terrorists' whereabouts. Mandy, as Saul, responded reasonably that he saw nothing because he had been hooded the whole time, the windows had been blacked out, and the cell phones Quinn seemed interested in were changed out every day. Rupert grew more heated over the dearth of information and amped up his interrogation, yelling at Saul and suggesting he wasn't trying hard enough. As Rupert's tone grew more strident and accusatory, Mandy responded with rage.

It was a natural response from a proud character who was already punishing himself for his mistakes and oversights. Mandy's choice, an outgrowth of how he understood Saul's character, felt justified and authentic. But it was problematic for me because it was wrong for this moment in the story. The story here was that Quinn is close to losing self-control. His zeal to capture Haqqani leads him to take outrageous risks in this and future episodes. This was the moment for viewers to understand that he was ignoring the human toll of his monomania.

Mandy is one of the most instinctive and sensitively attuned actors with whom I have ever worked, and his approach to his work is deep and internal. He has an unerring feel for authenticity and tremendous faith in the subjective impulses that arise within him. I was mindful of his way of working and knew that asking him to move off a choice that felt right to him — particularly at so heightened a moment — risked throwing a wrench into the performance. I appealed to him on the basis not only of *his* character's truth, but of what was right at this moment for the two other characters in the scene. This is something directors need always to stay alert to because it's not the actor's job to anticipate how their choices might affect someone else's storyline. That's *your* job. Your challenge as the director is to justify any adjustments you need the actor to make in a way that upholds the integrity of all the characters.

I pointed out to Mandy that it's not enough for Quinn simply to lose it in Saul's presence. The story point is that he continues his verbal assault when Saul is down, to the point that Carrie has to intervene to stop an unfair fight. If Saul were to meet Quinn's attack with the ferocity we have seen from him in the past — leonine and frightening — it might outstrip Quinn's own outrage and neutralize what we were hoping to establish. It also would render Carrie's intervention confusing and differently motivated. And it would not set Quinn off on his brave but reckless mission, with the audience beginning to understand just how possessed he has become.

I was grateful to Mandy for accepting this point, but I could sense that he needed a new way of thinking about Saul's mental state to justify a less reactive response to Quinn's assault. I agreed with his desire to remain true to his character and appreciated his commitment to absolute authenticity. What might we discover, then, to justify his being so nonreactive to Quinn's frontal assault? As near as I could recall, we had never before seen Saul lose his fierce self-assertion or belief in his powers. If Mandy were to play that Saul was now experiencing a true "dark night of the soul," if he were willing to touch the depths of depression, it would be startling and might add to the audience's experience of the enormity of the loss to which all of these characters have been subjected.

Mandy embraced this idea completely, giving so raw and beautiful a performance that Quinn's relentless attack allowed us to fear for both characters. Mandy fully absorbed this new dimension to Saul's character and added a lyrical touch when, in a later scene, standing naked in a running shower, water pounding down on him from above, he stared despondently at the floor. It was a poetic choice that could only have come from Mandy's fully inhabiting the devastated inner life of his character. What I understood, and have seen time and again in other situations, is that attention to story can focus an actor in ways that lead not just to appropriate action, but also to inspired choices.

MOTIVATION

A lot of fun has been made of the caricatured actor imploring, "What's my motivation?" But the truth is that this is one of the most fundamental questions to answer, for both actor and director. Drama is conflict, and competing motives or intentions drive dramatic interest. The actor has to know what their character wants, sometimes at several levels of the character's awareness. A character may think, for example, that they want to impress their boss, when at a deeper level it's really their father's approval they seek.

With an intention, actors have something actively to pursue — perhaps a desire they'd like gratified, or an outcome they want to bring about. And just as important as defining an intention is determining the obstacles in the way of accomplishing it. Those obstacles might come from society, from inner conflict, from the environment, or from other characters who have motivations of their own. Obstacles create the need for strategies, and the dramatic focus of most scenes is how different characters' intentions and strategies collide and play out. Helping actors find their intentions is critical in assisting them with their performance. One way to do that is to help them define their character's subjective state: What are their circumstances, history, assumptions about life, or even physical conditions?

Be specific. Avoid vague states or general intentions. A character doesn't just "like" or "dislike" someone for general reasons, but for very specific ones. Those reasons grow out of who the character most authentically is. You can help an actor find depth and complexity in each moment as it arises by exploring a character's desires, wounds, strategies, and aspirations.

One of my acting teachers was Stella Adler, whose most famous pupil was Marlon Brando. Stella broke with the Group Theater in the 1930s partly because of its emphasis on naturalistic acting. Yes, being "natural" is important, but it isn't everything. To make her point, she would stand before the class, slouch, pantomime smoking a cigarette, and then ask, "Is this very interesting? It's *real*, isn't it?"

Some actors rely on acting naturally, though they may simply be playing the surface level of the dialogue. They don't dig deeply enough into their character for a more interesting way to define what motivates them. When scenes don't take flight, it can often be because the actors haven't found bigger stakes or a more complicated inner life for their characters, thus missing the drama and depth potentially to be found in every exchange.

Stella would encourage her students to seek out large concerns, questions, or ambitions for the characters they played. She stressed the importance of making characters' inner lives full and rich, so that each moment they dramatize might spark interesting associations, both within the characters and for the audience. It's part of the director's job to help define what those larger stakes and more interesting backstories might be. If a scene involves, say, a mother with a teenage son who sleeps in all day and ignores his chores, an actress in the role of the mother might choose to play her dialogue as simply nagging her son to lighten her load and to help around the house. That would be understandable — natural, even. But how much would we care about either character?

What if the director gave the actress this intention? "I am worried about what we are becoming as a society; too many people are only out for themselves and are content to let others shoulder burdens that are rightfully their own. I want you to grow up to be someone who will make a positive difference by taking responsibility so that others can also thrive in the world." Chances are that even if none of the dialogue were changed, the viewer would sense the different issues being addressed and care a great deal more about both the characters and the newly defined story, which you, as director, would have enriched.

Motives and intentions can also assist actors in finding the emotional states a scene may require. If an actor is having difficulty accessing true sadness and perhaps even tears, for example, it may be helpful to suggest they enter the scene with the intention *not* to cry, *not* to feel sad. The effort to avoid feeling is sometimes the surest avenue to it, perhaps because it's easier to be overcome by troubling feelings than to actively invite them.

REHEARSAL

In series television, there generally isn't a lot of time for rehearsal. On a typical television episode, not only is there less time than when working on feature films. There is also the likelihood that your actors have just come from being fully immersed in another moment of the script, or possibly even a different episode entirely. When I start a rehearsal, I'll usually say a few words about what is at stake, perhaps reminding the cast of past events, some of which may not yet have been filmed. Before launching into a blocking rehearsal, I like to ask them all to read the words aloud, just to have them heard, not judged or "performed."

One reason for this is that it gives the actors a moment free from judgment — not just what they imagine mine might be, but also possibly their own. Another is that this might be the first time each actor really considers or "hears" the other characters' parts. Television schedules can be so rushed that actors often haven't the time to focus on the next scene, which could be embarrassing to admit. Pretending otherwise easily leads to inappropriate staging or performance choices that might take time to unwind. Simply reading the lines aloud gives the cast a chance to get oriented and makes it more likely that emerging impulses are grounded in story.

For most directors, rehearsal is a collaboration where the actors and director share thoughts about what feels right. The scene usually starts to come to life once it gets "on its feet," when the actors are free to move wherever their inner promptings take them. Where possible, I try to stay open and flexible as I watch the scene taking shape, wanting to see how it compares to what I've imagined. You might need to guide the actors back to a focus on story, or you may gain new insights you hadn't considered.

I generally like to help actors find physical activity in performing a scene. Often, the more embodied the performance, the greater the chance for genuine moments to occur. A physical task, where appropriate, can free an actor to access underlying intentions from a deeper, less self-conscious place, as well as to express those intentions in a more *embodied* way. Physicalizing deeper intentions not only helps the actor find the scene; it also assists the audience in understanding it, particularly in moments where behavior belies the characters' spoken intentions and reveals the subtext. The great thing about focusing on physicality is that it often provides a way to communicate something without actually saying it, and it allows actors to access the expressivity of their bodies.

I read that Francis Coppola once advised his daughter, Sofia, when she was directing her first film, to be sure always to see an actor's hands in any shot she framed. It's not just Italians who communicate through their gestures. The entire body speaks volumes. Dialogue is often expressed more naturally when an actor has something to do *physically* in a scene. Movement also activates the body, an exquisite organ of expression.

GIVING ADJUSTMENTS

Giving adjustments is its own art. It's hard not to take criticism personally, so it's important, as best you can, not to present adjustments in a way that could be taken as harsh or critical. You *want* the actor to make a choice about the material. The fact that you may disagree with it does not make you right and them wrong; it just reveals a difference of opinion. But you're the one entrusted with the storytelling. The challenge is to hear the actor's thoughts and adjust your own if theirs are persuasive, but not abandon your responsibility for how the story is told. The clearer you are in communicating what is compelling to you, the more likely an actor will want to collaborate and even be grateful for you deepening their experience of the role.

When adjusting a performance, I often start by acknowledging what I saw the actor doing in the previous take. I say this uncritically, simply demonstrating that I understand how they chose to play it. This helps the actor feel *seen*. They have probably given a lot of thought to the choices they made. If you simply dismiss the effort, it can be dispiriting for the actor. I then might say, "I'd like to suggest you think about this moment a little differently. Rather than making your strategy [x, y, and z], try intending to affect your scene partner in this other way." I'll try to justify the new intention by offering some imaginary circumstances more likely to point the actor toward where I think the story should be headed.

A benefit of this approach is that you have included the actor as a collaborator who is interested in what feelings might arise with a different intention and set of assumptions. You have not said simply, "Do it this way." If you had, you might get your desired result for that particular moment, but you may well have lost your actor's initiative and trust in their own instincts for the rest of the scene, or even for the entire show.

Directing actors is not a matter of one size fits all: Some actors don't do their homework; some have more depth of soul than others; some may be less present in the moment. You needn't be overly precious every time you deliver a note. But I do think it's better to err on the side of assuming an actor has invested some care in the performance rather than to assume a choice with which you disagree came from a lack of attention. In this way, you maintain a respect for the actor and their process. If it becomes clear that a particular actor is limited either in approach, temperament, or talent, then you must find a way to generate the correct inner state through less conventional means.

I recall a particular actor who was paranoid about any note that moved him off of how he'd planned to play a scene. He also was terribly narcissistic in his need to corral the audience's sympathy and pull focus to his character's personal turmoil. We were shooting a scene in which the actor was among a group listening to a beloved character reveal that she was suffering from a fatal illness. The moment was intended to be heartbreaking and to create empathy for her. The actor, hearing the news, went into a fit of sobbing that overwhelmed the moment. Knowing how difficult it would be to move him off his inappropriate choice, I tried this: "The more you contain your personal grief, and the more you demonstrate care for your friend, the more the audience will care about *you*." He took the note as if he had thought of it himself.

Another time, an actor new to the profession and unskilled in acting technique was floundering when he was required to make a dynamic entrance to a social gathering and be the life of the party. The actor himself seemed to be suffering from an attack of low self-esteem and simply could not access the appropriate confidence. The other actors — younger, but far more experienced — were brutal in the ridicule they heaped on him as he required take after take, unable to generate anything more than a depressed, cautious performance. The cast's derision was driving him deeper into his own gloom, yet I needed him to come in and electrify the party with his presence, good looks, and charm. After repeated failure to interest him in the backstory of his character, I remembered that the actor had been a stand-out college basketball player and had actually been selected in the NBA draft. I took him aside and said, "This is draft night. You've just been selected by the Los Angeles Lakers to play point guard in the NBA. Remember that feeling? Who you were when you went out celebrating that night? That's who's entering the room." He lit up, got in touch with something truly impressive about himself, and became the star the scene required.

If you want to adjust the mindset of the actor, try providing them with as specific an imaginary circumstance as possible. Usually there is something in the story you can draw upon to remind the actor of what their character's inner concerns ought to be. But you might need to extrapolate from the script in order to give your actor more to work with. For example, after an actor's character has learned he'd been passed over for promotion, you might suggest that, since that happened, his character has been unable to sleep or shake the anxiety that he's about to be fired. He's haunted that he'll be unable to make his next mortgage payment or pay for his children's education, and may even wind up homeless.

Specificity ought to play as much a part as possible when you suggest adjustments. What specific intention would you like an actor to bring into the scene? Active verbs are generally best. "I'd like you to *seduce* her," you could say, or *scare* her, or *make her feel sorry for you*, or *drive her away*. These are all examples of active verbs, which give the actor something to play and connect them to their scene partners. Simply telling them what to do or feel can disconnect them from the drama as it unfolds. At times, though, some actors don't need specific intentions as much as tonal notes. I remember James Gandolfini on *The Sopranos* once interrupting when I was trying to deliver a note on his intention. "You want it funnier?" he asked. "Yes, actually." And he immediately understood what to do and how to do it.

Concise notes are generally best. That's not to say you shouldn't engage in discussion. But a lot of talk can make an actor's eyes glaze over and put them too much in their heads. While many actors are highly intelligent and give a great deal of thought to the roles they create, the actual "acting" part of their job is usually not purely cerebral. They have to "get out of their own way" to allow their deeper resources to take over. Performances that are premeditated usually feel that way and don't engage the audience as deeply as those that seem naturally to just happen.

If you feel that an actor is giving an affected performance, the likelihood is that they have locked in to exactly how to play the scene, no matter what the other actor does. The director would do well to find ways to make that actor more engaged with their scene partners.

You might ask them to do an improv, just to shake the actor out of a rote performance. Or try varying the intention; that can sometimes move an actor off an over-rehearsed choice. If an actor isn't listening or responding to the individual with whom they're acting, the power of the scene will be diminished. It's hard to fake connection.

It's possible for actors to get stuck playing the same intention and not respond to how circumstances continually change with each response from their scene partner, or by new thoughts of their own. Wherever you notice your own interest waning in a scene, that's usually the place where more digging is needed. Burrow into those moments to discover subtle shifts in the dynamics that might flesh out and add texture to the interchange. Richer meanings may be unearthed by helping your cast explore what may be happening subtextually or between the lines. What would make each moment interesting to you and distinct from what preceded it? Perhaps the dialogue itself is the problem, in which case you might suggest it be changed or shortened. But more likely you and your cast haven't dug deeply enough to find a compelling dynamic between the characters.

Sometimes, it's smart to keep the camera rolling at the end of a scene rather than calling "cut," and to begin the scene immediately again while the actor is still in touch with whatever emotional release they have just experienced. Starting right away can result in more spontaneity because the actor hasn't had a chance to reset, which can lead to a premeditated performance. Deprived of a safety net, the actor's best alternative is to focus completely on their scene partner, which in itself can ratchet up the intensity and the life the actor is embodying. Some actors request successive takes without cutting because they know they will be more present after they have worked through the effort sometimes required to get "in" the scene. Once there, they can move about more freely and give expression to their impulses. This tends to work best after the story's beats have been fully understood. Then spontaneous emotional expression is somehow guided appropriately from the actor's deeper resources. Even when your intention is not to start the scene over again, it can be wise to keep the cameras rolling a little longer than usual because the most deeply felt moments sometimes arise after an actor has been freed from the obligation to prepare for the next moment. The scene might "land" after all the dialogue has been spoken.

Once the director is happy with the performances, I have found that it can be wonderfully liberating to offer the actors an opportunity to do one more take "for free." All the effort and desire to please can fall away because the performance has been safely delivered. The actor is freed to allow whatever impulses arise, which may or may not incorporate all the notes they have been given, but which often leads to a newly integrated and invigorating performance that really feels alive. A surprising percentage of those "free" takes find their way into the final cut.

In emotionally complex scenes, or ones that require the actors to experience particularly strong feelings, it can be helpful to remember that you don't need to ask an actor, in one slew of notes, to incorporate everything you'd like for the finished performance. It can be effective to allow an actor to explore the component pieces one at a time over successive rehearsals or takes. Patience with the actor can lead to a beautiful performance that integrates all that they have been allowed to explore.

In an episode I directed of the period Showtime drama *Penny Dreadful: City of Angels* entitled "Sing, Sing, Sing," I had a scene between the characters Tiago (Daniel Zovatto) and Sister Molly (Kerry Bishe). They were lovers from two very different worlds: he, a Chicano police officer dealing with racial prejudice in the culture and in his own department; and she, a radio evangelist, recruited by her mother as a front for the older woman's unethical financial exploitation of their followers. Both Tiago and Molly felt deeply compromised in their jobs, and the very existence of their relationship, if made public, would bring scandal.

There is a point in the story when they are each experiencing pressure in their private lives, but neither one feels able to share this with the other. They steal a few moments of refuge from their troubles, walking together on the beach. Molly suggests they go out for a night on the town, but Tiago points out the dangers of being seen together in public. She makes the case that they both need some fun, and, besides, maybe no one will recognize them. Charmed, he relents, and the two lovers excitedly make plans for their night out.

Because the show was "period" — set in the Los Angeles of 1938 — locations needed to be chosen that were correct for that time. The scene's beach house location, which included the shoreline where the couple would take their walk, was in an undeveloped spot on the coast north of Los Angeles. We wanted to keep the sand on the beach as pristine as possible to suggest that this was a remote area, so the two actors had to walk a few hundred yards to their start marks because I didn't want tire tracks left on the sand for our very wide master angles.

We waited to call for the actors until the sun was low enough in the sky to create a shimmering backlight reflecting off the ocean. This, however, put us in a bit of a time crunch to complete the scene before the sun fell too low. Because the scene involved a lengthy walk, the actors simply ran their lines before agreeing to go "right to picture" — shooting without a full rehearsal — both to preserve the virgin sand and because a stiff wind had whipped up, making communication difficult and playing havoc with Kerry's period wig and delicate wardrobe.

Daniel and Kerry are very talented actors and had developed deeply poignant screen chemistry. But the location presented a challenge that actors often have to deal with, which is to perform in less than ideal circumstances. They had to walk a great distance on sandy footing to a distant start mark, making communication with me and the crew difficult. They also were contending with a biting wind, potentially distracting them from their focus, and they understood we were in a time crunch. Pretty much all you can really do as the director in these circumstances is to stay positive, be understanding, and, most importantly, avoid getting distracted from the deeper layers — the meaning — of the scene.

We rolled three cameras, and on the first take, the scene felt natural enough. Daniel and Kerry delivered the dialogue accurately, and the plot point was made that they would spend the night out on the town. Their innate attractiveness and screen chemistry kept the scene compelling in its own way, but something vital was missing for me. As they took the long walk back to their start mark for the next take, with the sand being swept clean of footprints, I hiked over to them, organizing my thoughts as I approached. What felt off to me was that they had started the scene already connecting too much with one another emotionally. Tiago's opening remarks concerned how things were going at work for him and his partner. Molly responds supportively and asks what would be happening for them on Monday when they return to work. He mentions a ceremony in which he and his partner will receive a certificate of commendation for a crime they solved. Molly congratulates him, then turns the conversation to her desire that they go out and have fun, expressing how imprisoned she feels hiding out from the world.

The opening exchanges felt like small talk, simply a way into the scene before Molly brings up her wish for a night on the town. But I felt we were missing an opportunity, and the key for me was in their casual start to the scene. I suggested to Daniel that he begin more in his own private world, rather than relating to the woman at his side. He could be troubled by the great danger he and his partner were now in, which he must keep secret from Molly. I encouraged him to let himself be so distracted that he might not be very present at all. Her congratulating him for the commendation could drive him further into his misery because he knows what she cannot: that it's for a false accomplishment, and he is concealing wrongdoing of his own for which someone else is taking a fall. I mentioned to Kerry that if Daniel played those early moments as I was asking him to do, she should register his distracted mood, motivating her suggestion that they break out of their self-imposed prison to go have some fun.

We rolled again, with the wind still whipped up to near-gale force. The actors delivered beautifully, integrating my note into the performance. Though he could not admit to his anguish, Tiago's deep preoccupation set the tone of dread and loss of hope, which Kerry (as Molly) used as the reason to suggest the night on the town.

As the actors trudged back to their start marks, the assistant director asked if we might move on to the tighter coverage. This would be crucial for the later, more emotional moments of the scene, and the sun was continuing to dip. But something else needed adjusting, something that would be worth the risk, and I didn't want to move on yet because these wider angles were the ones I wanted to use for the early moments of the scene — the "beauty" shots that established the romantic setting and the context for all that was to follow. What was missing, I felt, was the same thing from Molly that I had asked of Daniel: less connection to her scene partner and more preoccupation with her own melancholy. While the previous take had given the scene more gravity, the adjustment I'd suggested needed to be built upon if it were not to have the unintended consequence of sacrificing Molly's inner life. She had become simply a caretaker of the man, trying to cheer him up. I reminded myself of the story and where it was headed. In the series as a whole, this was going to be a drama about a pair of doomed lovers, with Molly ultimately seeing no way out but self-destruction.

For the third and, I hoped, last wide take, I told Kerry that, while I did want her to register Tiago's emotional state, she should resist the impulse to caretake and instead let his mood remind her of her own fear for the future. She is actually concealing tremendous heartbreak and hopelessness and, like Tiago, is unable to share much of this with her lover. Suggesting the night out should be less motivated by wanting to take care of him and more in service to her own flailing, futile effort to calm the rising tide of her own alarm.

As I watched this last take unfold, I felt such appreciation for how Daniel and Kerry managed to summon from their own imaginations the meaning and truthfulness that made the scene come alive. The audience was cued to the greater stakes that gave depth to the story. They were invited to share in the felt experience of these characters, who were struggling under repression and the weight of living dishonestly. This made the seemingly mundane dialogue — none of which was changed — rich with subtext. The scene became invested with a fatalistic tone as the two lovers clung to one another, even while lost in their own desolation. When they turn to face each other, the water lapping at their feet, Molly redoubles her efforts to persuade Tiago to throw caution to the wind. Because of the emotional terrain she allowed herself to explore leading up to this moment, Kerry's pleading took on a heartbreaking undercurrent. Daniel, having touched the place of Tiago's pain, responds compassionately and, likely a little in denial himself, allows himself to be seduced by her proposed escape, which will end in chaos.

A director's relationship with the actor is a subtle thing. Sensing how best to make a suggestion — indirectly, or gently, or firmly, or choosing simply to "go again" without saying anything more — is as much instinct as anything else. I have found it fundamentally mysterious how communication occurs (or doesn't occur) when trying to elicit subtle shifts in performance. Directors would do well to appreciate the effect of *how* they communicate as well as *what* the gist of their note is expressing. What each actor needs will vary. You will have to read the person in front of you, as they are doubtlessly reading you in turn.

Most actors have worked very hard to develop a technique they may rely upon to help them deliver consistent and compelling performances. Your job is to help provide them with the conditions they require for those techniques to work. For actors less technically skilled, your job is more challenging, but no less essential: Find out what the actor needs in order to give their best performance, and then provide it. Some actors benefit from detailed reminders of where their characters are in the story or what intentions they hold entering the scene. Others need to be awakened emotionally, with the director suggesting imaginary circumstances, or asking them to recall times in their own lives that mirror their character's situation. Still others simply need space and time for their own process to unfold, and patient support while it does. Even then, however, the actor should know with certainty that the director is not just standing idly by, but is remaining deeply connected and mindfully attuned to what the actor is experiencing. The job is to park your ego outside and be supportive of their process.

CHAPTER SEVEN

STAGING
THE SCENE

O NE OF THE BEST PIECES OF ADVICE I ever heard regarding staging is to consider how viewers might understand a scene if the sound were turned off. If they only watched the behavior of the actors, would they be able to understand the scene's dynamics — what it was about, who was getting what they wanted, and its emotional tenor?

Much of this information is conveyed through facial expressions, but more is available through the ways the actors physically relate to their environment and to each other. And just as important as what the actors do is how the camera photographs them. When staging, a visual strategy has to be factored in as well.

My first television directing assignment was on a short-lived TV adaptation of the feature film *Fast Times at Ridgemont High*. I was directing a scene between two characters: one, the popular girl every boy lusted after; the other, a less popular guy who was self-conscious but wanted to ask her for a date. He approaches her at her workplace at the mall — the "hot dog on a stick" booth — and attempts some small talk. In the course of his fumbling, he says something that inadvertently sets her off into a jealous rage at the boyfriend he didn't know she had: His offhand remark reveals to her that the boyfriend has been dating someone else. The scene was comedic, intended to conclude with the boy understanding that he's not really a candidate for the girl's affections, and the girl being revealed as rageful and insecure.

I considered what the location offered that would give the actors some physical activity to help tell the story. I noticed that cooking the hot dog on a stick involved inserting a stick into a raw hot dog, dipping it in batter, plunging it into a deep fryer, taking it out when the batter had fried into a hardened shell, then handing it to the customer. It occurred to me that, since the scene was about the girl getting more and more upset, there was a possibility here to physicalize exactly what the scene was about. I staged it so that she would be dealing with another customer in line ahead of her would-be suitor. We'd see her perform the operation of preparing the hot dogs efficiently, maybe even a couple of times, as the boy begins to make small talk. As he gets to the head of the line and continues to speak to her, she becomes more and more upset, and her concentration on her physical task disintegrates. The scene ends with her in mid-rant, impaling a hot dog with a stick, inserting it into the raw batter, and handing him the uncooked mess. He stares at the batter dripping onto his hand as she is lost in her crazy revenge fantasy. Comedy allows you to stretch ordinary behavior because whatever the action may lack in plausibility is made up for in emotional truth. The staging came from taking advantage of what the actual location offered and asking the question, "How might I get the actors to engage physically with each other or the environment in a way that allows their deeper motives to be revealed?"

Other questions when considering staging might include: What is the dynamic of this particular scene, and what is it about? Is it contentious or harmonious? What are the key transitions, and how does it resolve? Does it represent a victory or defeat for any of the characters? At what precise points does each character either get what they want, experience frustration, or discover something requiring a change of strategies? Every scene is a kind of journey, moment to moment. The job of staging is to assist the actors in taking that journey and help the audience understand each story beat as it occurs.

Directing has been called "the invisible art," and with regard to staging, that's often exactly what it is. Sometimes, the most profound moments in a drama seem to just happen, without any apparent effort or manipulation. At other times, an unexpected staging might startle the audience into a particularly alert or emotional state. But all staging is a manipulation because through it — and the camera angles you choose — you're selecting exactly what and how the audience will see.

I almost always have a staging in mind when I approach any scene. Making a plan is part of the important prep work a director ought to do. Usually, the finished product is very close to what I have imagined. But it's preferable, I believe, if the actors feel they have arrived at a "blocking" themselves through what they discover in rehearsal. When actors feel trusted and validated in their choices — or at least heard if they disagree with you — the more likely they are to invest themselves in the performance. They are generally receptive to a director's suggestions, particularly if those ideas are grounded in getting to the heart of the scene.

Circumstances may arise when you don't have enough time to "find" the staging in rehearsal with the actors and will need to just implement your own plan. In most of those instances, actors are willing to adapt to the needs of production and make your suggested blocking work. They may ask you for an adjustment to solve a performance problem for them, and sometimes that is easily accomplished. But stay aware of all the story threads you're following. Story points can be affected by even subtle changes to the staging. You want your cast comfortable, but not at the expense of the story you're telling.

Since you're not filming a play being performed on a proscenium stage, you also have to figure out a plan for how to photograph scenes in a way that enhances the storytelling. The staging needs to work not just for the actors but for the camera as well. If it isn't possible to position the camera so the viewer can fully experience the story's key moments, the staging has failed in its primary responsibility: to affect the audience, not simply accommodate the actors.

In approaching staging, I think about what behavior would convey any power dynamics taking place in the scene, as well as what might help emphasize turning points. If one character is trying to persuade another, you could consider having them walking together, with the one making a case a step or two behind. The one in the lead becomes the object of pursuit. For a particularly loaded or confrontational moment, the characters might stop to face each other, cuing the audience that something is coming to a head. In a scene in which there is an argument, one character might sit down at the moment of defeat, physicalizing their "collapse." Or when a rejection has occurred, an actor might turn away from the other to return to some physical task, indicating that the conversation is over. These are examples of what you might suggest to help your actors connect to the dynamics of the scene. But they also point to what you need to consider in your prep period as you develop staging ideas.

Your job may be to determine how self-aware or deluded your characters are and how much their body language should reveal or conceal. There is artistry required in finding behavior that both advances the storytelling and is truthful to your characters' states of being: How much are they willing to show one another? How much is unintentionally revealed? Do they wish to communicate through their behavior?

One of the wonders of *The Sopranos* is how insightfully it depicts the complex and devious motives of virtually all the key characters. Despite their raw and elemental basic drives, they frequently behave self-protectively, fearful of being exposed for who they really are, as this could put them in great danger. The conflicting drives for safety and true expression are perfectly captured in the brilliant conceit of the mob boss seeking help in talk therapy.

In the fourth season, in an episode entitled "Mergers and Acquisitions," Tony and his wife, Carmela, are in the midst of trying to salvage their marriage. Carmela is well aware of Tony's past infidelities, but he has now committed to honor his vows. In this episode, however, Tony strays and sleeps with another woman. Carmela discovers this when she finds the woman's sequined fingernail extension in his laundry. She feels so betrayed that she steals $40,000 from Tony's "secret" stash in a backyard storage bin, fully aware that he will discover it missing the next morning. She also places the incriminating fingernail in plain sight for Tony so that he will easily infer that she has taken the money as a quid pro quo.

In the last scene of the episode, Tony comes into the kitchen, where Carmela is sipping her coffee. The story point at this moment is: She is challenging him to accuse her of stealing the money so that she can fully vent her enraged awareness of his cheating. He wants *not* to confront her, but does want to convey that he knows about the theft. He cannot win this battle if he challenges her, but he is determined to win the war by remaining in control. The dialogue is indirect, and thus it was incumbent on the acting and the staging to communicate the scene's meaning.

I don't recall my initial idea for staging, but once we started the rehearsal, James Gandolfini (Tony) had a strong impulse that he wouldn't want to get anywhere near Edie Falco (Carmela) because he recognized the threat she posed if she were to escalate to righteous fury. Physically expressing his intention to steer clear of her became the way he communicated his refusal to enter the trap she'd set. I was happy to embrace James' impulse, and we adjusted the staging to accommodate it. The staging deepened everything about the scene.

With Carmela seated at the breakfast table, Tony avoids eye contact with her by walking into the kitchen but staying far from where she is seated. When she stands and approaches him to make the coffee she offered, Tony crosses against her and repositions himself at the opposite end of the room. In conventional coverage, the director often tries to position the actors so they might fit easily within a manageable "master" angle. James' idea was challenging in that it required much wider coverage to capture the physical distance between the two characters. It became apparent very quickly that the strangeness of his character's movement was the perfect "play" for Tony to communicate the meta-message of the scene: He was not about to cede position to Carmela, no matter what his transgression. He would find his own ground, pay the price she'd exacted, and never admit to anything. Also, the physical space between them perfectly represented how they each recognized the other as a formidable adversary. The very wide angle required to capture them both helped to create a sense of the scope of the battle.

As the scene took shape in rehearsal, I saw an opportunity to let the camera reflect the power dynamic between the two. The opening frame featured Carmela powerfully in the foreground, her back to Tony as he comes down the stairs to the kitchen. He looks small behind her as she matter-of-factly offers coffee, reads the paper, and doesn't look at him. She holds all the cards and doesn't need to push her advantage, knowing he will eventually need to address what happened to the missing $40,000. And when he does ... well, hell hath no fury. Using a wide-angle lens both to empower Carmela in the foreground and to minimize Tony's size in the background, the camera wheels around Carmela to show Tony moving behind her, across the entire width of the room and into the kitchen. He travels from the camera-left side of Carmela to her camera-right side while the shot keeps her in the foreground, dominant in the central position. She is the hub of the wheel, and Tony only a smaller rim-dweller in the background, still trying to figure out how to wrest back control from his formidable wife.

The staging communicates that Tony is starting to find his footing when he accepts Carmela's offer to make him coffee, requiring her to rise from what had begun to seem like a throne at the breakfast table. As she approaches, perhaps expecting to move in for the kill, Tony surprisingly crosses against her and positions himself at the opposite end of the room, leaving Carmela by herself in the kitchen making coffee. From this point, the two are "equals" visually until the end of the scene, when Carmela returns to her seat while Tony remains standing several feet from her. By not ceding anything, by feigning ignorance in response to all of her pointed questions, he ends the scene still on his feet, standing apart from her. He has avoided getting caught in her trap and being weakened by having to admit his infidelity. Carmela has to settle for sitting smugly in the knowledge that Tony knows he has, for the moment, been bested. But there is also the faint sense of disappointment that she still has not won the war, which neither of these formidable adversaries will ever be able to do. The story is in the staging, as it should be in as many of our creative decisions as possible.

CHAPTER EIGHT

REWRITING THE SUBTEXT: *THE AMERICANS*

As the director of an episode of television, you sometimes feel as though you're arriving late to the party. You do all you can to connect to the story, identify elements within it that interest you, and find themes you care about. Often the script itself, or what the showrunner or writers share with you, is enough to generate the understanding you need to do your best work. Sometimes you have to explore below the surface of the material to find something that compels you about it. In either case, you want to emerge from prep knowing the purpose of each scene: what it's meant to dramatize, how it fits into the larger story, and what is going on within each of the characters.

But what about those times when you have finished your prep and are still in the dark about how to make a particular scene work dramatically? The writers or showrunner may not share your concerns, or they might simply have moved on to other episodes. What then? Filming will still have to begin, and once the scene is shot, that will be it until you get into the editing room, where perhaps the scene can be restructured and improved. But by that point, your fixes are likely to be only Band-Aids.

In fairness, a writer's reluctance to rewrite has at times, in my experience, proven wise. Stories can work in ways that are not always easy to anticipate. But you must value your own instincts and keep pushing for clarity. It can make a difference. Even when you don't get the rewrites you'd like, you can always ask: How might I capture something fresh and truthful in this scene? How could I adjust these performances so that they feel like interesting human behavior? How can I bring this to life?

I directed several episodes of *The Americans*, a wonderful six-season series from showrunners Joe Weisberg and Joel Fields. The series depicted the razor's-edge lives of two Russian double agents posing as a suburban Washington, D.C., couple, the Jennings, during the Reagan era of the '80s. What made the show so compelling wasn't just the espionage, but the way it dramatized how honest human communication is often compromised by private agendas. The conflicts between characters were astonishingly subtle, complex, and real. It sometimes took me a while to identify the deeper layers on which an episode's story was operating, so I was not surprised to be a bit confused on early reads of scripts, particularly when new subplots were being introduced.

Joe and Joel were responsive showrunners when it came to my questions in the tone meeting for my episode, "IHOP," in the show's fifth season. One scene in particular seemed to need more reason for existing than justified by what I saw on the page. That year, part of the dramatic focus in the lives of the Jennings, played by Keri Russell and Matthew Rhys, involved the departure of veteran KGB handler Gabriel (Frank Langella). Gabriel was a calm, understanding presence for Russell's character, Elizabeth, but was occasionally at loggerheads with Philip (Rhys) over conflicting ideas of moral service. Philip is having deep second thoughts about having committed atrocities in the name of a political ideal and is considering alternative, maybe even spiritual paths. He is painfully evaluating whether or not he can continue his crippling indentured servitude to Mother Russia. This inner struggle has contributed to a crisis in his marriage to Elizabeth, who is intolerant of what she views as Philip's self-indulgence. Recently, relations between the couple have begun to thaw. But now that Gabriel has left the country, a void has been created not just for Philip and Elizabeth, but for all the other operatives whom Gabriel oversaw. They, too, are suddenly without their handler.

Opening the second act of the script, we are introduced to Father Andrei, a Russian Orthodox priest, who waits on a hospital bench. He is soon joined by Philip, wearing a disguise. They have an oddly specific greeting, suggesting they are using coded passwords to verify they are both spies for the same team. This greeting also makes clear to the audience that these two have not previously met. Father Andrei delivers a report to Philip in which he earnestly provides intelligence that is difficult to follow, mostly because it concerns other priests we know nothing about. Having absorbed the report, Philip excuses himself and starts to leave. Father Andrei stops him to ask if he'll see him again. Philip says it's doubtful; another handler will likely be assigned to Gabriel's former operatives. Father Andrei persists, saying he may have useful information to report and that Gabriel said it was important they talk things through. Philip again politely declines, and Father Andrei says that he'll pray for Philip, who is unimpressed.

Then Father Andrei suggests Philip try prayer, as he must lead a stressful life. Scene.

Directing can sometimes feel like holding a line of string at either end, with the art being to grasp it just loosely or tightly enough to keep the audience engaged, knowing when to relax it and when to pull it taut. The audience will follow your thread if the story is well-conceived and you manage the tension carefully. But if you drop the string entirely, it's very difficult to get the audience's full attention back. I felt that was happening here. This scene seemed odd and confusing, with no groundwork for it having been laid and the audience asked to follow a complex debriefing about characters they didn't know. I imagined there might be a payoff in future episodes, but, even so, the scene stuck out like a sore thumb in an otherwise excellent script. I felt it had no dramatic tension or compelling questions for the viewer — other than, perhaps, "Why on earth did I just spend my time watching this?"

The tone meeting was my chance to ask the writers what this scene was really about: Why was it in the script, and what did it contribute to the story? "Well," Joel said, "we wanted to show that this is how the KGB worked. Russian Orthodox priests were recruited to spy and keep tabs on one another in exchange for being permitted to practice their faith outside the Soviet Union." Joe and Joel were nothing if not diligent about their attention to Cold War realities.

The research was impressive, I acknowledged, but I was still wondering if this two-page scene was meant to be more than a historical footnote. "Is any of the intelligence Father Andrei provides going to lead to some operation?" Negative. "Are we establishing Philip as his new handler?" *Nyet.* "So Philip is performing a one-off, and none of the information he gathers will be paid off in later episodes?" Right. "And what might Father Andrei's intention be in this scene, since I'll be having to direct him?"

"Gabriel was Father Andrei's only friend since, as a spy among his peers, he had to dissemble with everyone else. Father Andrei wants to form a friendship with Philip because he has lost Gabriel."

I wasn't terribly happy with that as the subtext because I feared it would make Andrei's character rather pathetic and difficult to care about. I understood the poignance of the historical reality, but I didn't see the contribution that this dynamic between Father Andrei and Philip would add to the drama.

At last, Joe said, "Well ... we also need to introduce this priest because in the next episode, Philip's going to recruit him to perform his official Soviet-sanctioned marriage to Elizabeth."

Finally, I understood why this had felt like such an uphill battle. It wasn't for this episode that the scene existed; it was to establish Father Andrei so he would be available for his important function in the next one. That function had nothing to do with his qualities as a character, but only with his being a priest. The wedding sequence would be a momentous event in the life of the series, and I fully understood that I had to do the best I could to introduce Father Andrei in a way that somehow felt organic to the episode I was directing.

The day arrived when we were to film the scene. I rehearsed with the two actors, sharing with them the subtext that had been recommended in the tone meeting: Philip was there as a temporary substitute for Gabriel and wanted, essentially, to get in and get out. Father Andrei was nervous about the change in handlers, wanted to make a good impression, and in particular wished to bond with Philip as a possible friend and confidant. We ran the lines a few times and staged some action, Philip standing to leave and Andrei rising in an effort to delay him with a last entreaty. The scene had an almost pathetic quality to it. Philip looked pityingly upon the priest, whose offer of friendship was futile and far removed from the larger concerns of Philip's life. He felt sympathy for the priest's situation, but didn't have the time or inclination to befriend the man.

The positions were marked, the crew started lighting, and the actors went to finish getting ready. I was unhappy. I told myself what one usually does in these situations: "Not every scene is going to be great. Maybe the audience won't notice that nothing much is happening." But I didn't believe that. I knew that in fifteen or twenty minutes the actors would be called to set, and the scene would be committed to film, for better or worse.

Still, I couldn't help exploring what the scene might be about if I considered it differently. What bothered me most was the abject quality of the character of the priest. He had been completely neutered. I understood that this was intended as an indictment of the Soviet system, which routinely did that to the people it controlled. But that didn't make him a dramatic character. The actor playing Father Andrei (Konstantin Lavysh) was an impressive-looking man, tall and stately with deep-set brown eyes and a soulful countenance. I thought about why Father Andrei had become a priest in the first place: He is a spiritual man; his work is to provide comfort and spiritual counsel to his congregants; he offers compassion and insight, bearing witness to their struggles. *That* would be a character I could care about. Then I thought, what if, instead of having betrayed his calling, he is actually in the process of performing it? What if he were coming from a spiritual perspective in this very moment and responding to what he senses in Philip's soul? I was immediately intrigued, no longer dealing in my imagination with a broken character, dependent on others.

But was that in the dialogue as written? I looked again at the lines and was struck by what Father Andrei said about Gabriel: "I used to just tell Gabriel things and ... (beat) ... he always said it was important for him that we talk them through." Up until this moment, I had understood those lines as Joe and Joel had told me they were intended: Father Andrei was appealing to Philip to be his friend. But the phrase "important for him" caught my attention. Frank Langella's Gabriel had a deep and soulful presence. What if he had gone through a crisis of faith similar to Philip, but we never knew it? That's not hard to imagine, given how thoughtfully Langella played the handler. Gabriel was willing to not adhere strictly to Soviet procedures and would cut Philip slack for his periodic rebellions. Gabriel wouldn't have been able to discuss his soul-searching with anyone else — not Philip, whom he had to keep on the straight and narrow, and certainly not any of his superiors, who would possibly send him to Siberia. Father Andrei would be the perfect and safest choice — the only one, really — with whom Gabriel could share self-doubts and perhaps even spiritual longings. I also liked the added dimension this gave to Gabriel's character and how it felt surprisingly appropriate for a man of his sensitivity.

It struck me that this could be a *fantastic* moment. What if this priest had actually intuited Philip's spiritual crisis, but couldn't be so bold as to come right out and say it? He would have to communicate obliquely — with subtext — in order to give Philip a safer way to consider his offer of friendship. In telling him of his meetings with Gabriel, he could be subtly conveying to Philip that Gabriel had come to him for relief and counsel, and he was inviting Philip to do the same. This flipped the priest's intention and became far more interesting: It's not that Father Andrei wanted Philip to become *his* friend; he was offering Philip the chance to make a friend and spiritual advisor of *Father Andrei.*

If Konstantin, the actor, were to hold the intention of wanting to communicate *this* to Philip — between the lines of his last-minute appeal — he would no longer be experienced as pitiable but as wise, sensitive, and compassionate. More importantly, he could elevate the moment into a rare glimpse into Philip's soul. That would depend upon Philip's response, so I returned to the script.

There was an interesting stage direction, simply that Philip "looks at Father Andrei" before responding with, "I'm sorry. I just can't meet with you on a regular basis." Stage directions don't always need to be followed; most writers understand that actors and directors will find the best ways to stage a scene. But in this case, giving Philip a moment to size up Father Andrei was ironically exactly what was called for, though not as it may have consciously been intended by the writers. I had no doubt that if I gave Matthew the note to infer that Father Andrei had intuited something Philip was trying to hide, he would use the scripted beat to convey his surprise and fear of being exposed, justifying turning down the offer of counsel. Then, with a little reassurance from Father Andrei, he might soften to the idea. The dialogue supported this shift, as Father Andrei expresses understanding, as well as his intention to pray for Philip. The final line has Father Andrei saying, of prayer, "It's a great solace. Especially when you live this kind of life." What had felt somewhat hapless now carried the ring of unexpected warmth and compassion.

Fortunately, this had all revealed itself to me very quickly, still with time to implement it. I could see that almost no staging adjustments (or relighting) would be necessary. There was one slight adjustment I wanted to make so that Father Andrei might step very close to Philip for his last line, to underscore the deeper meaning he wished to convey. But this could easily be accommodated.

The actors took the note, and I could sense their palpable relief at getting to play intentions that gave life and stakes to the moment. When the scene played for the cameras, after Father Andrei's last line referencing the solace that fans of the show know Philip so desperately longs for, Matthew's stillness is broken as he visibly swallows, a physical expression that speaks volumes. The actors nailed it.

The changes not only greatly improved the scene; they also established a more meaningful connection between Philip and Father Andrei, lending significance to Philip's decision in the next episode to ask this man to perform the wedding service. I was very happy not just to have improved the episode under my direction, but to have assisted in the telling of the story going forward.

There have been other scenes in my career that did not lend themselves to this sort of thorough overhaul, or for which I simply lacked the ingenuity to see how to elevate them. But what I hope is illustrated here is that the shifts in the scene did not depend on a rewrite. Not a single line was changed. Yet the scene had the feel of having been rewritten because what is significant is intention and subtext. The adjustments occurred to me not because I departed from the story, but because I immersed myself in it and remembered its overarching themes. That's what made me confident the writers would have no problem with my looking beyond their suggested subtext.

I think it's worth noting that what emerged as an entirely new interpretation began by noting one detail that bothered me: the abject quality of Father Andrei's characterization. My instincts rebelled at pinning a whole scene's interest on such a beaten-down character. By honoring the detail that speaks to you — being curious about why it either bothers or excites you — a journey can start that will lead you to discovery. This is actually a valuable lesson in all manner of creative explorations, and it's certainly so in directing. Notice what detail nags at you. It may be your entry into the story.

A footnote here is that, upon concluding the scene, I called Joe and Joel to share my excitement about what we'd discovered in filming it. They of course knew of my frustration with the sequence and were actually thrilled, not just that I was finally happy with the scene, but that we had deepened and enriched it. As excellent showrunners, they had the show's quality foremost in mind, not ownership of particular moments.

Ownership is itself a tricky subject, and I truly feel that the collaborative process invites all of us to reconsider the very idea. If the scene hadn't been written precisely as it was, with Father Andrei saying of Gabriel that it was important *"for him"* that they meet regularly, I don't know that my reexploration would have even gotten started. That the dialogue between Philip and Father Andrei lent itself so seamlessly to the deeper interpretation leads me to believe that, somewhere in the writing process, the writers were operating at the same, albeit unconscious, level that fed me. To their credit, Joe and Joel didn't claim that they'd known this subtext had been there all along. But it's a great example of the power and mystery of collaborative creativity. We bring our own perspective and abilities to the work, and if we stay fiercely committed to making something great, or at least truthful and dimensional, exciting discoveries can be made.

CHAPTER NINE

THE LANGUAGE OF CAMERA

A DISCERNING EYE CAN BE SOMETHING ONE IS born with, or it can be developed through study, effort, and experience. Being willing to learn from those with whom you work — even seeking out people who have expertise you lack — can be richly rewarding. As you learn from films you've seen or directors of photography with whom you work, it's important also to remember that the thing you can't learn from anyone else is how *you* see, how *you* feel, how an image or composition strikes *you*.

I learned that lesson during an early experience with a director of photography who, for some reason, had no interest in being helpful. I was still new to directing, and he may have resented that he hadn't been given my episode to direct. He seemed to resist any ideas I had for how to position the camera or what lenses I preferred. I was frustrated, but willing to consider that I had something to learn from this veteran of many shows. Other cameramen with whom I would later work did indeed contribute greatly to my knowledge, but this one seemed to have other motives. We struggled through the first few days of shooting; then we came to a sequence in which a crime boss was to arrive for a meeting with his associates. I staged a master shot in which the camera dollied along one side of a long conference table, moving parallel with the boss as he walked down the other side, passing his henchmen, who greeted him obsequiously. The camera stopped when it met the boss at the head of the table where he sat down in profile, facing right toward his lieutenants, who then took their seats on either side of the table. I thought it was effective to "shoot through" his associates, introducing them and establishing the important man's arrival.

The DP didn't express any concerns or objections. But when it came time to shoot the coverage (those additional angles on individual actors, or smaller group shots), I indicated that for the boss's angles, I wanted to position the camera so that he'd be facing squarely toward the lens, looking either just left or right of the camera depending on which side of the table he was addressing. The DP proclaimed that it could not be shot that way because "it would not cut," meaning it would cause problems in the editing room.

"What do you mean?" I asked.

"Well," he said, "you've just shot a master establishing everyone to the right of the boss. And you have to honor the screen directions established in the master angle."

"You're telling me," I asked, "that my coverage of the protagonist in the scene has to remain in profile so that he always looks to his right?"

"That's correct. It follows from the master angle you designed, and you can't jump the line you've established."

Had this happened to me now, I can only imagine how I would have responded. In fact, there are several ways to get around the issue he raised, even within the "rules." But at the time, I was inexperienced in visual communication and insecure when it came to screen direction, which refers to which side of the camera subjects should face when seeming to look toward their scene partners. Strictly speaking, if one looks to the right, the other should look to the left. I feared that if something "didn't cut," it meant the whole sequence would be disorienting and incomprehensible. Also, this DP was far more experienced than I, was something of a tyrant with his crew, and was the darling of the showrunner.

Feeling thrown, but aware we had to move forward, I agreed to start shooting in the way he had stated I must. We first filmed the henchmen, which wasn't so problematic because, depending on which side of the table we pointed at, the camera could be moved to give each character a "tight eyeline" to the boss; when they appeared to be looking at him, they needed only look slightly to the left side of the lens to satisfy the DP's concern. The camera would capture all of their facial reactions of fear and desire to please. But I felt sick when considering where I felt forced to position the camera for the boss. For him to have to always look to the right side of the camera, I would need to keep it in almost the same place where the master shot had landed: in profile, which would prevent the audience from feeling the full force of his intimidating presence and, by extension, the sense of how his lieutenants experienced him. I simply couldn't get over the fact that something was terribly wrong. I would be denying the audience a full experience of the moment, leaving them unprepared for the rest of the story.

The crew had already struck the lights for the first side of the coverage and were in the process of lighting the reverse angle on the boss when I realized I simply could not proceed, no matter the consequences. I told the DP and assistant director that we would have to reshoot the first side of the table so I could "split" the eyelines of the henchmen to match how I would shoot the boss's split look. I would be jumping the line in order for the scene to play the way I wanted it to.

All hell broke loose. The DP screamed that I was wrong and would be putting the company into OVERTIME! He called the show-runner to tell him I was ignoring his help, and the reshooting would not be his fault. Presumably, he also told him the scene *wouldn't cut!!*

I can't say I felt secure about what I had done. My expectation was that there would likely be a price to pay for my insurrection. But I can say that a great weight lifted, as I no longer felt I was betraying the story. I feared I might not live to film another day, but I would tell the story the way I saw it.

This was one of many instances, particularly (but not only) early in my career, when I needed to trust my story instincts over concerns that I might offend someone else's sensibility or anger others who thought I didn't need a certain shot or additional take. It can exact an emotional price to assert your position in the face of others' judgments. I'm not advocating being indifferent to those concerns. Sometimes they're merited. But until you fully accept your role as the primary storyteller, you may be confronted with the choice of either abdicating your position or proceeding half-heartedly. It's okay to question your choices in the face of disagreement from your collaborators and to change your mind if another's sugges-tion makes sense. But take responsibility for the story you're telling. You're the one who's been entrusted with the job.

That DP's concern feels almost quaint now, as screen direction nowadays is frequently ignored — sometimes too much, for my taste. But the important thing about that experience was that it started me on a road toward honoring my own vision. Rules are helpful, but too slavish an allegiance to them can do damage to originality and artistry. You don't want to lose the forest for the trees, the forest being the emotional or subjective experience you're working to give to the viewer. I've never heard someone say, "Wow! I loved that film. It followed all the rules!" Rules are useful when they assist with communication, not when they get in the way of it.

There will be times when an intuitive leap beyond the rules can catapult the viewer into startling and transformative experiences, opening up new depths to the story and maybe even resulting in those same rules being rewritten. The French New Wave director Jean-Luc Godard edited his film *A Bout de Souffle* (*Breathless*) by jumping his hero from one moment in the action to several beats in the future, making for a subjective state in the viewer somewhat matching that of the playful, adrenaline-junkie protagonist played by Jean-Paul Belmondo. What became known as the "jump cut" is now a staple of film editing that, when appropriate, can transform storytelling and at the same time reduce the number of shots required for a particular sequence.

Your relationship to the camera will evolve over time, and the subjective states you understand the camera can create will influence what you see in your imagination. The very lenses you choose to employ can themselves create associations or connections that serve the story. I recall the excitement I felt when I first learned to appreciate the difference a particular lens can make when shooting a close-up. If I used a "long" lens (think telephoto), I'd get a more flattering look, softening the actor's facial features. This can be great for romantic moments or when a more idealized image is called for. I'd also be isolating the actor from much of their environment because the shot would narrow the field of view in the background, and focus would be restricted to just the face. If I shot the same size frame on the actor with a wide lens (requiring the camera to get much closer to the subject), there would be more detail and three-dimensionality in the facial features — less flattering, perhaps, but creating the sense in the viewer of being physically closer to the actor. Viewers might feel more personally affected by the actor's behavior, as if they were right there in the scene with them. The wider lens can be less comfortable or more intimate, depending on the dramatic context. Also, with the wider lens, viewers likely experience the actor being more *in* the environment, with a much wider swath of the background visible in the frame and in sharper focus. The longer lens, on the other hand, might be appropriate for a spy or surveillance story, since it suggests the character is being watched by someone far away. Which lens is appropriate for a given scene depends on several factors, but primarily on what experience you're hoping to create for the viewer. Your lens choice will also be affected by, among other things, the visual style of the show you're working on, where the moment falls in the life of the story, and your own aesthetic sense.

Attention to the felt quality of each moment is crucial to good storytelling. What feeling state would you prefer to induce in your viewers to best prepare them for what is to follow? Intrigued? Calm? Disturbed? If a surprise or shock is to come, you don't want to tip your hand. Or you might want to exploit the ability to instill a sense of anticipation in the viewer for a feared or longed-for outcome. Perhaps it might be a moment for the audience to take a breath and relax after a particularly intense sequence. Even then, however, there is a visual component to consider: What image would elicit restfulness or feel unobtrusive? Sometimes a particularly beautiful frame enhances the experience of the story, while at other times it may diminish tension you're working to generate. Once the story has started, *you're always in it.* Don't forget that. The two ends of the thread are in your hands, whether pulled taut or held loose. Just don't ever let go of the story; it's hard to get back.

In the finale of the third season of AMC's *The Killing,* there was a grand reveal of the identity of the serial killer, whom the show's protagonist, Detective Sarah Linden (Mireille Enos), had spent the previous two seasons tracking. The killer turned out to be her mentor and lover, Senior Detective James Skinner (Elias Koteas). The series was marked — visually and otherwise — by an oppressive moodiness, reflecting both a dark worldview and Sarah Linden's internal state. One interesting visual feature of the show's "language" was to film *through* things, obscuring the frame with foreground obstructions, like reflective glass or rain, or framing the actors within foreground objects, circumscribing the characters. This is an excellent example of creating a visual experience that exactly mirrors the show's themes: in this case, a world in which the characters must penetrate layers of appearance, either to know each other or to recognize themselves. The style also communicates the ways we can be hemmed in by circumstances or history, and the difficulty of ascertaining "the truth."

With the reveal of Skinner as the killer, I wanted to create as much shock as possible and also suggest how traumatic this is for Linden: For her, it's actually a *retraumatizing* of a previous defining wound. The reveal happens when she and Skinner are caught leaving his home by his estranged wife and their daughter.

After looking daggers at Linden, who visibly shrinks into herself, Skinner's wife huffs off to the kitchen as Skinner tries to reassure his sobbing daughter that things will work out. It's excruciatingly uncomfortable for Linden, whom I pinned in position halfway up a narrow staircase, unable to move until Skinner and his daughter, at the foot of the stairs, resolve their moment. They cling to each other in a desperate hug, with Linden looming slightly above them just a few feet away. I staged her there so she would be caught in as claustrophobic a situation as possible, forced to confront her guilt for adding to the distress of this family. I also shot a "push-in" on her through the profiled father and daughter, who were in soft focus in the foreground. This cued the audience that the drama at this moment was not so much about father and daughter; it was about Linden, trapped and wishing to be anywhere else in the world. *That* was the story, or at least what I wanted the audience to think was the story.

As Linden tries to avert her eyes from the parent and child, whose relationship she has likely fractured forever, she sees the left hand of the daughter, which is wrapped around Skinner's neck in an embrace. On it is a distinctive ring with a large blue stone: This is the key piece of incriminating evidence that Linden's team has been trying to track down ever since they discovered it was the one item missing from the body of a murdered teenaged girl. Only the killer could have taken it. It's a moment so jolting to Linden that all color drains from her face. I hoped that by misdirecting the audience into a different story expectation — Linden's descent into her own misery and guilt — they, too, would experience a shock for which they were completely unprepared.

The moment breaks, Skinner's daughter departs, and he holds the front door open for Linden so they might continue toward her car parked out front, Skinner carrying the suitcase he had just packed in order to move in with Linden. She is frozen in horror as she fully realizes she has been in a relationship with a true monster; then she moves, zombie-like, past Skinner, who is embarrassed by the uncomfortable confrontation with his wife and hurriedly overtakes Linden to load the car. My challenge: How to photograph Linden in a way that would create for the audience all I wanted them to feel was happening within her?

The human response to trauma is often to freeze, to emotionally depart from the body and retreat to an alternative reality. I thought viewers might share in this response if, within the shot of Linden moving down the walkway, the image shifted into slow motion. Her internal landscape was changing; she (and the audience) was experiencing time in a new way, from a different state of being. The ambient noise would also drop away, creating the opportunity for an otherworldly sound design to take over and further remove Linden from the present moment. Mireille's performance was haunting, and I wanted the audience to feel an intimate connection with her, as this was the deepest reveal yet in the entire three-year run of the series into the nature of her trauma. I asked her to look straight into the lens as she moved toward Skinner. This would break the so-called fourth wall and give the audience the feeling that Linden was looking directly at *them*. The viewer would be in Linden's turbulent inner world, where she feels unable to take in the enormity of the evil that has enveloped her. The next cut revealed that her look is at Skinner, the back of his head bobbing up and down, also in slow motion, as he continues his march to the car.

The script indicated that this moment for Linden was made more disorienting by her confrontation with the banality of evil. She is trying to absorb the understanding that this level of depravity could coexist with the most mundane, even innocent of circumstances. As Skinner walks toward the street, I wanted something to enter the shot to motivate the camera (now established as Linden's surreal point of view) to pan with it and off of the killer, objectifying her inability to hold focus on the immediate crisis. I needed a vehicle of some kind, moving left to right across the frame, enabling Linden's view to move with it. I chose an ice cream truck, which I felt perfectly captured Linden's desire to retreat to an innocent time and allowed for an ominous sound effect: the universal, tingly melody summoning children to come for a delicious treat. Linden's view (and ours) shifts off of Skinner and moves with the truck as it glides by in slow motion. It clears the frame to reveal a swirling sprinkler head (which I had asked the special effects department to strategically place there), spraying water in slow motion and contributing, I hoped, to the hypnotic state in which Linden is perhaps seeking refuge. Then a young boy on a bicycle (another image of innocence) enters from the right of the frame, pedaling back the other way. The camera pans with the boy, dropping us off again at Skinner. Still in slow motion, he turns to look directly into the lens, as if to Linden, but putting the audience in his crosshairs. Still assuming Linden knows nothing of his true identity, he pauses before we cut back to Linden, who now — finally — gazes upon him in full horror and disgust for who he is. Skinner looks at Linden, and in that very moment registers that she knows. He shrugs. I chose that moment to ramp the cameras back to normal speed, with the rest of the scene playing out as cop moments generally do. Linden approaches to cuff him, back to inhabiting her high-functioning detective persona.

What I love about this sequence is the way the visuals tell the whole story, without any need for dialogue. The actors did a brilliant job of communicating their inner life, but the camera (beautifully supervised by DP Greg Middleton) took their subjective experience to a whole new level. By distorting the experience of time, by breaking the fourth wall, by putting the audience into Linden's point of view, and by cuing the viewer as to which story to follow, the camera was speaking as only it could, allowing for a rich and visceral experience. Not every visual choice you make needs to be "dramatic," of course. It can diminish the impact of your work if the visuals call attention to themselves for no real or apparent reason. Some of the camerawork I most admire is relatively undramatic — it simply places the viewer in exactly the best position to experience the story as fully as possible. What's most important is that the camerawork be appropriate for the particular moment in your story.

In Chapter Five, "What Story Are You Telling?," I discussed an episode of *Northern Exposure* entitled "Buss Stop," in which a character named Michelle (Teri Polo) has recently arrived in the community and volunteers to direct a local theater production of William Inge's play *Bus Stop*. She is a fish out of water in a new world and naïvely thinks to herself, "How hard can this be?"

The story would work best, I thought, if the audience were invited into the feeling of things spinning out of control. I liked the idea of the camera seeming to have a life of its own, as the events themselves do, no matter how much Michelle is determined to control them. I felt that a Steadicam, swirling around her as she checked on the various cast and crew members preparing for the show, would give viewers a sense of the dizzying experience she was having. As things spiral out of Michelle's control, the camera itself becomes uncooperative, moving off of her intended path and toward someone defying her instructions. At other moments, the camera's swift movement slams to an abrupt stop as Michelle is met by crew members demanding attention. This visually mirrors her own stalled efforts as opening night fast approaches. When the performance finally takes place, the camera becomes "quieter," inducing a more hushed sort of experience for the viewers, as if they too are in the audience watching the play. This is very different from utilizing the camera arbitrarily, or because it feels "cinematic."

On an episode from a different series, I once had an uncomfortable experience with a director of photography who advocated using a similar visual scheme for a scene in a way I thought would detract from the story. That scene took place in a bar, where three young characters were playing pool. Two were boys and best friends, and the third was the ex-girlfriend of one of them. The former boyfriend had already assured his friend that he wouldn't care if the friend tried to move in on his ex, which is what he proceeds to do, cozying up to her to demonstrate how she might hold the pool cue. The story point was the growing jealousy in the ex-boyfriend as he watches the friend place his arm around his former girlfriend. The way I imagined it would be edited was to intercut between increasingly tighter shots of the ex-boyfriend and angles on his friend charming the ex-girlfriend. The DP, an excellent but temperamental cameraman, had expressed enthusiasm for having the camera circle around the action nonstop, creating a dynamic and exciting shot. Scorsese's *The Color of Money* was the reference the cameraman cited to justify his choice. It surely would be exciting and dynamic, I told him. But it would also work against the moments I felt were most important to emphasize at this point in the story. The DP was more of a "star" on the show than I was, and I tried to be as deferential as possible. But I stuck to my guns because I could not incorporate his suggestion in any way that made story sense to me. Feeling rebuffed, he took great offense and retreated to the camera truck, never to reappear for the rest of the scene. His lighting crew had to make their best guess as to how to proceed, and we completed the work without him. It was awkward and unpleasant, but in the editing room, I had no doubt I had made the right decision.

It is critical to consider point of view when selecting camera angles. The camera communicates whose scene it is. Are we most interested in how events are affecting one character in particular? If so, your framing can help your audience to understand that. A convention in shooting coverage, for example, is often to "match" shots of each character. That is to say, if you have a 50mm lens shooting over the shoulder of one character, you should use the same lens shooting over the other character's shoulder when you reverse angles. This is thought to allow for a more seamless flow in the editing process. Often, this is true. But if, for example, you want to cue the audience that one character is having a more isolated internal experience than their scene partner, you could suggest this by *not* matching the coverage. You might choose instead to shoot the more isolated character in an unobstructed single, without the back of the other actor in the frame. The audience would see one character alone and one not, suggesting these two characters are experiencing themselves and this moment differently.

You can also convey story points in the way you choose to frame your characters' eyelines to one another. I directed an episode in the first season of the Amazon show *The Boys* entitled "The Self-Preservation Society." *The Boys* offers a subversive take on a thinly disguised version of the Marvel Cinematic Universe, essentially turning it on its head. The superheroes are mostly depicted as deeply flawed human beings, dependent on the corporation that markets them to cover up their violent excesses and make them appear to the public as altruistic and heroic. In fact, they are serving only the interests of the unscrupulous corporation, which controls everything they do. "The boys" are underground insurgents dedicated to unmasking the true nature of the villainous superheroes and bringing them and their corporate overseers to justice. My episode included the backstory of the leader of "the boys," Billy Butcher (Karl Urban), who throughout the season has demonstrated a ruthless desire for vengeance for some unidentified event from his past. In a flashback, we see that Billy's wife, Becca, has disappeared under mysterious circumstances, which has sent him spiraling into grief and depression. He is visited by a woman, Grace Mallory (Laila Robins), who claims she has information on his missing wife. Suspicious, Billy sits on his sofa, waiting to hear what Grace has to say. She places a laptop in front of him and starts to play security videos of Billy's wife. He stares at it, transfixed, as Grace brings him to understand that, just before she disappeared, Becca was sexually assaulted by Homelander, the most powerful superhero of all. Horrified and in shock, Billy asks, "Who are you?" Grace displays her CIA credentials and answers, "I'm the person who can get you payback."

In approaching how I would film this scene, I considered what might deepen the audience's experience of Billy's brooding state and the depth of his wound. Grace was positioned beside him, and for her coverage, I placed the camera so that she would have a tight eyeline to Billy. Her gaze toward him would be very close to the center of the camera. He is her only focus, so it felt right that the audience would experience her full, laser-like power as she speaks to him. But for Billy's shot, I thought it more emotionally accurate to keep the camera's position closer to the point of view, so to speak, of the laptop on the table because that is where his real emotional involvement is. By framing him in profile when he looks at Grace but straight-on for those moments he turns back to consider what he has just learned from the laptop, I hoped the audience would understand his subjective experience: the terrible grief that seals him off from real connection to others.

The vantage point from which you choose to film your actors can help to create not only the point of view through which they are perceived, but also what the characters themselves are experiencing. In this case, I was less interested in Billy being seen from Grace's POV than in giving the audience a window into his internal state. Only when Grace promises him a chance at vengeance by saying "I am the person who can get you payback" did I feel it right for the audience to experience Billy from Grace's point of view. She had finally pulled his attention away from grief to the new purpose she was giving him. The only angle of Billy I shot from Grace's perspective was his tightest close-up, to be used precisely at the moment she "turned" him. If I had shot any of his looser coverage from there, it might have found its way earlier into the cut before I wanted the audience to feel that Grace had pulled Billy into her orbit. Only at this last moment has she finally captured Billy's attention, unleashing him to pursue his dramatic quest for vengeance. Through the visuals, the audience is subliminally guided to experience both Billy's inner state and the moment his new objective is born.

Framing also includes consideration of the relative height of the lens. If you position the camera lower than the actor, so that the point of view is looking "up" at the character, you're putting the viewer in a more childlike perspective. This gives the character more of an air of authority and power. Alternatively, looking "down" at actors can make their characters seem less intimidating or authoritative. The audience might feel invited to evaluate them less emotionally, almost as if from an objective perspective. This was a convention often employed in *The Sopranos* when Tony sat in therapy with Dr. Melfi (Lorraine Bracco). Like other directors of the show, I always made sure to shoot a high angle looking down on Tony for those times I wanted the audience to view him as a floundering everyman rather than the frightening mob boss he embodied at other moments.

Among the many other ways the camera can affect an audience's inner experience is to deprive them of visual information they very much want to have. This can help to build tension or anticipation. In a wonderful documentary, *Visions of Light*, William Fraker, director of photography for the psychological thriller *Rosemary's Baby*, described how director Roman Polanski asked him to set up a point-of-view shot for Rosemary, the expectant mother played by Mia Farrow. Her sinister "friend" (Ruth Gordon) goes into a bedroom off the hallway to take a call from the obstetrician from hell (Ralph Bellamy). When Polanski returned to direct the shot, he went to the open bedroom door and closed it just enough to conceal everything but the back of Ruth Gordon's head, so that the audience (and Farrow's character) wasn't able to see any part of Gordon's face. This puzzled Fraker until he saw, during the film's first public screening, that precisely at that moment, the entire audience shifted suddenly to the right, as if to peer around the partially closed door, anxious to get more information about what might be revealed from the muffled phone call. If they hadn't been fully invested in the story before, they certainly were then.

Giving thought to how you intend to edit a scene can help you determine how to position the camera. Is it the kind of sequence that might play in one shot? If so, you might consider incorporating more camera movement to sustain the viewer's interest. Do you feel the scene ought to be cut in brief, rapid rhythm, requiring several shots from different angles, either to disorient the viewer or to spike the scene's energy? If it's an intimate scene, do you think it would play best in close-ups? How, in the editing, will you want to "contextualize" the moment? With an extremely wide shot, in which your characters are dwarfed in relationship to the world around them, or perhaps simply with a shot just wide enough to frame the actors so the viewer feels close to the dynamics taking place between them?

If you don't consider how you'd like the scene to be edited, you're likely to miss out on a whole dimension of the storytelling; your shot selection will, in all probability, be random and general. I'm not suggesting that you should necessarily lock yourself into a particular cutting pattern; once you get into the editing room, the story itself may evolve and shift emphasis as it's edited. What worked rhythmically in the original conception may not work so well if the episode is shortened or reconfigured. But it's still important to have a sense of how you want your scene to cut because that will inform many of your decisions regarding camera movement, number of shots, composition, and even lens choices.

Don't simply shoot every actor from every angle with every size lens and assume it will all get sorted out in the editing room. This is not only frustrating for the cast and crew; it can also result in getting everything *but* the one imaginative, artful, surprisingly appropriate shot that is the product of knowing what you're communicating. In an episode entitled "The Unflinching Spark" on the Hulu show *Chance*, Hugh Laurie, playing the title character of this noir thriller, was attempting to rescue his lover from the sadistic control of her sociopathic husband. I had a scene in which Chance breaks into the apartment of the absent husband to search for evidence to use against him. Hugh's character was an introspective and self-protective man, terribly intimidated by the husband, a corrupt cop who had already physically threatened him. As Chance searches the apartment, he finds no clues revealing the husband's character or where he might be vulnerable. The script indicated that, when Chance enters the cop's bedroom, he sees an altar dedicated to the image of the wife, with pictures of her from various moments in their relationship. It's intended to awaken the hero to the obsessive nature of the husband's attachment to his wife and also add mystery to the wife herself who, in the photos, seems to present a different persona from the one Chance believes he knows.

In conceiving the shot for this reveal, I asked myself what would be a surprising, even shocking way to find the altar, the better to emphasize the game-changing escalation of stakes? How would I be most jarred, were I the viewer? Were I the hero? I designed a shot that followed Chance as he entered the bedroom, staying on his back as he moved to the opposite wall, against which was a king-size bed. As he moved to a bedside table, the camera came around to the bed's opposite side to see Chance's face as he considered the bed where his lover and her husband had lain together. The audience has by now seen three of the four walls in the room, having essentially been in Chance's point of view. My hope was that they would not feel deprived of any significant visual information, and that Chance's troubling reverie gazing at the bed would give the audience a feeling that the scene's reason for being had played out. He then turns back toward the door, preparing to exit. The camera pans on his head turn to become his point of view — and ours — of the last unseen wall, where the altar on the dresser is set.

To make the reveal more shocking, I asked the art department to plaster most of the entire wall with a dizzying array of seductive and alluring photos of the wife, who had clearly posed for them in a manner she seemed to enjoy, suggesting mystery in her relationship with the abusive husband. It's a shocking moment for Chance, *and for us*, as he understands in an instant that the cop is more obsessed with his wife than even Chance is, jolting him into doubting his own ability to successfully challenge so maniacal an adversary. It also causes him to wonder whether the woman who posed for those pictures might, in true noir fashion, be playing *him*.

Another factor to consider when you direct an episode of any series is the sensibility you're entering. What has the audience seen in past episodes? Rejecting the established visual language of the series might jeopardize what you think you're communicating because the viewer is likely to have visual associations that you may be ignoring. In the 1990s, the show *NYPD Blue* created a sensation for shooting almost entirely in a handheld mode. The camera was never stabilized by being affixed to a dolly or tripod, and instead shook slightly with every move the camera operator made getting into position or trying to find the correct framing. The "language" thus created gave this drama an immediacy and a feeling resembling a documentary, in which nothing is planned, no outcomes are known, and anything might happen. In contrast to that style, the brilliant HBO series *Six Feet Under* utilized proscenium-type, wide-angle still frames, both to create a classic feel and also to suggest the final stillness of death, a central theme of the show. The visual template also included a signature shot in virtually every episode: Using a split diopter lens, the focus was kept sharp on objects at different depths of field. The emotional impact highlighted particularly significant moments, inviting viewers to consider multiple meanings. You can choose to depart from a show's visual template, but that should be a conscious decision with your full understanding of how the audience is likely to experience your deviation from the norm. This needn't necessarily be regarded as a limitation. Accepting a show's visuals as a language to learn can actually open up new opportunities — not so you can mimic it, but so you can then speak it *in your own voice*.

The Wire is generally regarded as one of the very best television series ever created. Its depiction of American culture and society is complex and disturbing, and serves as a disruptive corrective to the myths Americans have historically told ourselves about who we are. Everything about the show is astonishingly powerful, from the writing, to the performances, to the overall production. And that includes the visual language that was established in the first season. One of the things I most admired about the show was the way it treated each character as a unique soul who deserved to be seen in their full complexity. Creator David Simon allowed for dignity in all the characters, including those often marginalized or seen as threatening to polite society. It's telling that scenes were shot in a style that contrasted markedly with the handheld, shaky camera used in most "gritty" dramas at the time. Rather than trying to create a sense of alarm in the audience, or suggesting that these characters were purely threatening and lacking in basic humanity, *The Wire* would often film drug dealers and drug users with a constantly drifting camera in an elegant, wide frame. At times, it seemed as if the way the drama was filmed might as easily have been applied to a stately, British period drama. The effect for me was to convey — through the visual language — that these characters had the rich complexity and potential dignity of any other, more traditionally "worthy," subjects.

Learning and embracing that visual language took me, as director, to the very heart of the show. In the world of *The Wire*, we are invited to reflect on the society that shaped these characters and consider how people can be weighed down by forces not of their own making. In this way, the show illuminated for its viewers their shared humanity with the characters, and also, perhaps, their shared flaws.

In directing *The Wire*, I imagined scenes with this drifting camera in mind. The visual idiom provided a rhythm, setting a mood for most scenes and becoming a useful tool in focusing the audience's attention. The camera might switch from drifting side to side to slowly pushing-in or pulling-away in order to support moments that might otherwise not have "landed" as well for the viewer. Simply freezing the camera's movement altogether can become another device to arrest attention and heighten a particular moment.

The Wire's third season dealt with how the police addressed a drug problem that was destroying neighborhoods. In the episode I was assigned, entitled "Straight and True," a high-ranking police officer, Major Colvin (Robert Wisdom), devises a plan to segment off an abandoned portion of the city and allow the drug trade to operate freely within it. The hope was that this would enable nearby neighborhoods to be freed from the toxic impact of the drug trade, resulting in far less violence. Colvin has to pitch the idea to the mid-level drug dealers to convince them to set up shop in the zone newly dubbed "Hamsterdam." In keeping with the visual style of the show, I arranged the dealers in a semicircle around Colvin and kept the camera drifting circularly around them as he makes the case.

In the following season, I was given an episode entitled "Margin of Error" that dealt with the public school system and its treatment of the impoverished neighborhood children. Colvin had been fired from the police department for his involvement with Hamsterdam and has landed a job as a field researcher with the school district. At one middle school, he and the principal decide to remove the disruptive students who are sabotaging the education of the well-behaved ones and place the offenders into a single classroom, where they might rise or sink together.

As the misbehaving kids are introduced to their new classroom, it falls to Colvin to explain the new rules to them. I saw an opportunity to create a visual callback to the previous season, where Colvin was in a similar position, appealing for cooperation from the distrustful drug dealers. I arranged the classroom desks so that they would be in a semicircle, the same way the dealers had stood in relation to Colvin in the third season. I used the same circular camera moves as in the previous season's episode, creating a visual link between what was happening here and what had happened the year before. The issue was similar: a law-breaking sub-group within the greater population was making things difficult for the law-abiding others to function. If this sub-group were segmented off into their own environment, the others would have a better chance to thrive. In this instance, the delinquent kids themselves might get a chance to start over on better footing.

With the visual callback, I hoped to remind viewers how the previous "social experiment" had turned out: an idea that might have borne fruit as an imaginative solution to an intractable problem was undermined by people in authority who cared only for their own narrow interests. In addition, there had been no institutional support or political will to take responsibility for addressing the scourge of the drug trade. I hoped that a reminder of that missed opportunity might add to the poignance of the current season's story and its focus on the vicious cycle that condemned generation after generation of children born into the drug culture. Would a tragic fate befall this difficult but talented group of young people? Their only hope was for their unique gifts to be discovered and valued. The visual callback created an association that I hoped would help viewers deepen their understanding of the story and point them to empathy for the human beings it portrayed.

One of the great opportunities of being a visiting director in series television is the chance to enter so many different worlds and see things from new perspectives. In the series *The Marvelous Mrs. Maisel*, the visual language is sophisticated and a crucial part of the world of the show. The shots and staging sweep up the audience in a journey of wonder and fancy. Highly complex scenes are often filmed in one continuous shot filled with visual jokes to delight the viewer.

I directed an episode in the show's third season entitled "It's the Sixties, Man!" and approached the assignment aware of the high bar set by the showrunners and primary directors, Amy Sherman-Palladino and Dan Palladino. I began by looking for sequences where I might contribute the sort of visually charged moments that are so much a part of the show's appeal. The writing, as usual, provided many of those opportunities by creating zany characters and rapid dialogue. (The Palladinos' scripts evoke for me the films of Preston Sturges. If you've never viewed any of those brilliant comedies from the 1940s, please treat yourself!)

One of the storylines in my episode concerned a group of beatniks taking over the Maisel household, their numbers multiplying in successive scenes like unwelcome spores. They are introduced in an early scene in which Midge (Rachel Brosnahan) exits an elevator and moves down a hallway toward her family's apartment while chatting with a nosy neighbor. As she enters the Maisel apartment, she finds her father, Abe (Tony Shaloub), with three young people draped on the sofa. In keeping with the visual style of the show, I wanted to have this all play in one continuous shot. This required some sleight of hand to enable the Steadicam to follow Midge from the elevator, down the hallway, through the doorway, then come around her to see the door close before panning her into the living room to reveal phase one of the beatnik invasion. I found that the hallway dialogue with the neighbor played slightly too long to keep Midge on the move throughout, something I wanted to do to keep the scene energized. Maintaining energy is vitally important, both to the show's sensibility and to sustaining the single shot. In following Midge and staying in her point of view throughout the long Steadicam shot, I felt the humor would be heightened by saving the first cut for Midge's surprised reaction at seeing the beatniks in her home. Rachel Brosnahan — quite expert at solving this sort of problem — figured out a way to slow her progress by a few halting moves, which gave her and her scene partner time to complete their dialogue without stemming the flow.

The following morning in the episode, we see that the beatniks have stayed up all night, having ransacked the place of almost all provisions. Abe's attorney (Max Casella) is also there, preparing Abe for an upcoming legal battle. Ignorant of Abe's legal problems, Midge enters, exhausted and exasperated, having been unable to sleep through all the racket. She confronts her father, then is interrupted by the lawyer, whom she has not yet seen and who represented her in a previous legal skirmish. There is a hilarious "Who's on First?" type of exchange before Midge takes Abe away to speak with him privately.

In preparing for this scene, I was stuck on how credible it would be for Midge not to notice the lawyer (whom she knew well) while he is conferring with Abe. I asked Dan Palladino, who wrote the episode, if we might add an exchange to justify the lawyer exiting to the other room to fetch some papers just before Midge enters. This would enable him to reenter from her blindside as she challenges her father. It would also position Midge between Abe and the lawyer as she looks back and forth to them in confusion, heightening the physical comedy. Dan obliged, and that was how it was staged. That done, the challenge was, again, to establish the household chaos in a single shot. I chose a circular Steadicam move that started on the beatniks smoking and eating, then arced around Abe and his attorney engaged in their legal maneuvering. The move ended in an almost total reverse from where it had started to reveal a bedraggled Midge emerging from her bedroom. The master played well in one shot, although I did shoot coverage angles in case we might want to highlight particular moments. In the finished cut, we did in fact make use of those angles for some of the later moments. But the energy for the scene's comedy was fully realized by the care with which we took to nail the master.

The third beat in this storyline was, for me, the most fun and challenging. Midge returns to the apartment later in the episode to discover the place now completely overrun by seemingly all of Greenwich Village. Beatniks are everywhere, laying waste to the exquisitely appointed apartment. Midge is further affronted by a female Marxist acolyte who has taken to ordering around the Maisel housekeeper, Zelda (Matilda Szydagis), as if she were her own servant. Midge moves through the crowded apartment to find an overwhelmed Abe. She informs him that the visitors are using his bathroom, which sends him caroming down the hall. Just then, Midge's estranged husband, Joel (Michael Zegen), enters with their two children, and Midge has to pry Zelda away from her new "boss" to attend to her real responsibilities. It's a beautifully conceived scene and offered many opportunities for both great comedy and visual flair. My job was to create a shot that would contextualize the comedy, lead the audience through a kind of Alice-in-Wonderland reveal of the chaos, be in the precise right spot to sell each joke, and sustain Midge's point of view and the shot's entertainment value long enough to give the audience the feeling of being on a magic carpet ride.

In order for jokes to land in a sequence like this, you must make sure the audience's eye (the camera) is in exactly the right place at the right time. It would help, for most of the jokes, to stay in Midge's point of view, giving the audience an opportunity to be in her subjective state before registering her entertaining reactions. Midge's movements (and therefore the camera's) would need to mimic the energy of the story beats, some of which would be swirling and chaotic, while others would be abrupt stops. Holding one continuous shot for as long as possible was the goal. I started on a few of the invaders near the apartment doorway as Midge entered. I didn't want to show much of the party too soon because I felt it would be more fun to see it through Midge's eyes. But I also needed to contextualize what she was walking into, which was why I staged some action before she entered. The first scripted dialogue came from the beatnik who had taken to ordering around Zelda, which, since I wanted to be in Midge's point of view, she would need to see. This meant there would be a dialogue gap between her entrance and the orders to Zelda, a gap that ran counter to the style of the show. I asked Dan for help in providing dialogue I could give to a different beatnik. I felt some impassioned political position coming from an unfamiliar "guest" would add to the comedy, giving Midge a longer journey toward total incredulity as she makes her way through the apartment. Dan mentioned budgetary considerations if we added another speaking role, so I suggested we give the new dialogue to a character who had already been cast to speak at another moment later in the scene.

Next, Midge would need to observe the young woman giving orders to Zelda, but I also needed her in position to cast a glance down the hall toward Abe's bathroom door so she might plausibly know that the interlopers were using his bathroom. Rachel moved to the proper vantage point for both observations, justifying the move by physicalizing her worried fascination with the chaos around her. The camera's view ended over her back to see down the long hallway. That also positioned her (and us) to see Zelda approaching from the kitchen before being confronted by the entitled Marxist. As that beatnik turns to walk back past the camera, Midge follows, allowing for the camera to begin what was to be a full 360-degree turn, tracking Midge the long way around through the dining room, into the living room, then back to the front door just as Joel and the children arrive. In simply following the action, the camera gave the audience — through Midge's point of view — a reveal of how completely the Beat Generation had taken over the family apartment.

To sustain interest in the shot, I enlisted the help of the assistant directors to give the many extras entertaining and outrageous bits of staging, demonstrating their rapacious takeover of the environment. I requested and received from Dan more dialogue for previously established characters so that we could see them voicing self-important and comic palaver as Midge passes by. Rachel added some great character bits to enhance the timing needed for the move. One of these was to race ahead to pick up an ashtray, then return to thrust it into the hands of one of the yammering beatniks whose cigarette ash was about to drop to the floor. The beauty of her choice was that, in addition to helping the camera move, she physicalized her character's desperation to prevent further damage to the apartment.

The camera continues its swirling motion to reveal something new to Midge: a spontaneous hootenanny taking place around the fireplace. At a total loss, she calls out for her father, revealed by the continually turning camera as he emerges from his office, also filled with beatniks. I wanted that room to be packed, but the shot had already burned through all thirty-five background players we hired for the scene. The solution was to reuse the extras seen earlier in the shot. They would move off to new, later-to-be-seen positions once the camera had panned off of them. The effect was to add to the total number of bodies the audience would feel had descended upon the apartment. Coming from his office, Abe joins Midge, who asks him about the banjo player just coming into view of the panning camera and motivating the scripted line of outrage from Abe: "This is a banjo-free zone!" When Abe learns of the invasion of his bathroom, he storms off with Midge following, thus motivating the camera to complete its 360-degree turn back toward the front door for Joel's and the kids' arrival. There was yet more to the shot, but I think you get the idea.

These are only three of the sequences in a show that calls for similarly complex, imaginative camerawork in almost every scene. In this way, *Maisel* creates an entire world enhanced, of course, by a variety of other complementary factors, such as vibrant colors, dazzling wardrobe, perfectly coiffed hair, and energetic performances without which the vibrancy of the visuals would fall flat. The heightened reality invites viewers to engage from a similarly playful aspect of themselves, facilitating their ability to enjoy the fun.

By way of contrast, I had an equally exhilarating experience directing a show that couldn't have been more different visually from *The Marvelous Mrs. Maisel*. *Friday Night Lights* rarely played scenes (or even lengthy sections within them) in a single shot. The visual feeling of that show was documentary-like, and the strategy was to position three cameras on all sets while the actors, who did not rehearse, roamed wherever they liked and were pretty much free to change dialogue or mismatch from previous takes in the hope and expectation that what would emerge in each take would feel real. Whatever planning one did as the director was best kept to yourself because the actors were always encouraged to be in the moment and to follow all their impulses. The resulting behavior always felt like "real people" captured in stolen moments. Camera operators would rarely anticipate movements, even if they actually knew they were coming, so as to maintain the feeling that this was "really happening" and couldn't have been foreseen. The interesting camera angles audiences came to expect from the show resulted, more often than not, from the three camera operators having to find frames that avoided seeing the other cameras. This helped to create the subjective state in viewers that they were watching something real.

After just a few takes of each lens size on one side of the eyeline, operators would flip over to the other side so that the characters would be facing each other opposite from where they had been in the prior shot. The resulting footage would be a jumble of mismatched shots, generally resulting in an exhilarating cut sequence for airing. The job of the director was primarily to sense when the feeling of the scene had been realized, even if all the dialogue hadn't been exactly stated or delivered at all. The approach felt a little like jazz, almost completely improvised, and often resulted in fresh moments that would have been hard to achieve in any other way. (Rarely, by the way, are showrunners and writers as willing to let their carefully crafted scripts be altered so dramatically as the actors and directors were able to do on this show. I believe the gamble more than paid off.)

Not all series, of course, have as unique or as specific a visual language as these do, but a show's visual idiom is something the episodic director always has to consider. I am drawn to anything that might offer me a new way to see the world, as this challenges me to break free of old patterns that may have become desensitizing. A fresh outlook is enlivening, so long as it's connected to something truthful and revealing about human experience. That is the gift and the challenge of having to tell a story from the inside out. At first you may feel like a foreigner to the conventions of a series, but it's your job to understand and absorb them so they become the filter through which you learn to view experience and to tell the story.

A series' visual style, or language, can evolve over time, and if you're in the position of working on a show in its early stages, you might have more power to influence it. On the first season of *It's Always Sunny in Philadelphia*, I was hired to direct the last three episodes, although they eventually aired in a different order. The full season was only six episodes, so I was prepping while the first block of three episodes was being shot. I was drawn to the show because of the amazingly fresh vision and talent of the three main stars: creators Rob McElhenney and Glenn Howerton, and Charlie Day. Kaitlin Olsen later added her comic gifts, and the inimitable Danny DeVito joined the troupe in season two. As I watched the first episodes being shot, I was struck by the way these performers' strengths were being confined and limited by the conventional way the episodes were being filmed. The camera would face one direction covering the entire scene, and then the company would "turn around" to shoot the other side, requiring the actors to match exactly their same actions and performances. This is how most shows are filmed; however, it seemed to me antithetical to the free-form energy Rob, Charlie, and Glenn had captured in their $250 homemade pilot, which had gotten the attention of FX studio chief, John Landgraf. Based on that pilot, he took a flyer on them, and this turned out to be one of the shrewdest business and artistic decisions in the company's history. At this writing, the producers are readying their fifteenth season.

I decided that, for my three episodes, I would shake up the visual style to better accommodate the actors' talents and their zany, unpredictable energy. It seemed to me that the humor often depended on the precise, moment-to-moment connection among the actors, and that the slightest variation in one performance produced a unique and compelling response in the others. Having to split apart the performance into separately shot angles often sacrificed that electric energy and inhibited the actors' freedom to unleash creative impulses that this particular comedy thrived on. Though much of what appeared to be improvised was actually scripted, the subtleties that arose from take to take varied greatly. Capturing both sides of an exchange at the same time was the only way I could imagine doing justice to the sparkling comedy.

I asked the director of photography, Peter Smokler, if he might be able to light each set in a way that would permit shooting in a nearly 360-degree radius. This would permit the actors to roam more freely and allow multiple cameras to work simultaneously in opposing directions. The goal I set, which Peter made possible, was to film each scene in its entirety, with all actors being "covered" at the same time. I was sure this would free them in ways I had not observed in the earlier episodes. Shooting with simultaneous cross coverage meant not having to recreate spontaneous moments, which rarely feels quite so spontaneous.

This approach also made inventive staging possible, which became a hallmark of the series. Similar to what *The Marvelous Mrs. Maisel* later did in a more stylized way, the camera operators on *Sunny* worked out a choreography for themselves in which they could hand off coverage to one another as actors moved about the set, in and out of different cameras' frames. Rehearsals would involve the operators strategizing to ensure that some camera would always be capturing every one of the actors. Frequently, staging required more than one camera setup because there might be the need for tighter coverage. But we always tried to work things out so that all the coverage for a particular lens size was handled in one take, both cameras shooting across from one another. Not only did this liberate the actors, allowing them to express any comic impulses, but it also created a unique relationship between the audience and the "eye" of the show — the documentary-like lens, not always reliable, through which all was seen. The audience feels almost like part of the gang as it watches the characters inevitably succumbing to their baser impulses and hilariously paying the price.

The actors loved this form of shooting and suggested inventive ways to take advantage of it. The visual gags worked much better when they were incorporated into a flowing camera and were often not dependent on a cut. Also, the energy was more kinetic because the actors always knew their performance counted, and so they delivered much more for their scene partners to react to. There's just more adrenaline that courses through performers when the camera is on them. The set became so free flowing and creative that it remains for me a highlight of sheer fun.

Whether you're working within prescriptive visual styles like *The Marvelous Mrs. Maisel* or *Friday Night Lights,* or something you have more freedom to define, the camera is always crucial to the story-telling. The greater the rigor with which you approach the story, the more expressive you will discover the camera can be. Visual imagery communicates in ways similar to poetry, creating complex associations and states of being that put the viewer in just the right place to be most affected by the story. It can even point the viewer to where the meaning of the story lies.

If you do the work of identifying how you'd like to see your story — identifying what images come to you when you put yourself imaginatively in each moment — you'll have the makings of a visual plan. For me, it also helps to spend time alone on the locations themselves, giving myself the opportunity to feel how they speak to me and to see what imagery arises when I "dream" the story right there. Quite often, the image that feels most appropriate comes from the camera operator or director of photography, who might show you a camera position or lens choice that perfectly captures, or even enhances, your sense of the scene. But always remember to ask yourself: How does this choice make me feel? If the eyes are the window to the soul, your camera is the window into the world and the soul of your story.

CHAPTER TEN

MAKING IT MAKEABLE: *SNOWFALL*

W HENEVER I'M GIVEN A NEW SCRIPT, I first read it with no intention of figuring out how I will approach any particular sequence. I simply want to let it wash over me as if I were the audience. At the end of that first read, I try to analyze how and why I was affected, where I was drawn in (and where I wasn't), what interested me, and what I felt the episode was about. I then begin to consider individual storylines, each character's arc, and what interrelationships there might be among the various plotlines. I try not to limit my imagination with any production concerns. Until I have determined how best to tell the story, I won't really know the challenges of shooting the script or whether it can be done within the budget.

One of the adjustments I made when I became a director was to stop being an assistant director. By that I mean I stopped trying to immediately identify anything that would require special attention or resources: Which sequences might take extra time to shoot?

What special equipment might the director want for a particular scene? How many extras will be needed? There are countless other details that an assistant director needs to consider when scheduling an episode and making it shootable within budget and time constraints.

All of those considerations ultimately are within the purview of the director, but not necessarily from the get-go. The director is hired not only to be able to bring the shoot in on time and budget, but also because of their vision; hired, in other words, to dream, to fantasize, to make their mind as unfettered as possible in order to tell the best version of the story. To do that, the director needs an open channel to the imagination, needs to be fed by resources that are not necessarily pragmatic or even conscious. That openness and curiosity become constrained if you are worried whether or not it's okay to do something ambitious, time consuming, or "not sensible." In all likelihood, there will be a time for reining in the imagination. But settling too early for what appears to be doable is generally a prescription for pedestrian work. You're shooting a story, not a schedule. Few people are rehired solely because they brought a show in within the budget. As director, you're the X factor that can bring added value to a production depending on your talent and your unique storytelling instincts.

When I was hired to direct the opening episode of the third season of the FX show *Snowfall*, I was presented a script that included an ambitious opening stunt sequence on the streets of South Central Los Angeles as well as a sprawling nighttime shoot-out, a shocking murder of one of the recurring characters, a barfight, an aerial stunt sequence culminating in a crash landing on a Mexican airstrip, a grand-opening celebration, the rekindling of a romance between two lead characters, a lengthy nighttime driving sequence ending in a nightmarish reveal of a crack house, plus many other highly charged sequences. It was a well-written, densely packed script, and it promised to be a great kickoff to the season. But it was huge.

As a show for basic cable, *Snowfall* does not have the budget of *Game of Thrones, The Marvelous Mrs. Maisel,* and other premium cable or streaming shows with opulent production values. Yet it's aiming to capture a similar number of viewers and strives always to compete by intelligently marshaling its more limited resources. This, frankly, is the challenge most shows face. Even those with far greater resources try to contain costs so that they don't exceed the budget. This can make the job of directing series television sometimes feel like pulling off a magic act.

For this season-opening episode, I wanted to give the producers every possible story beat they had envisioned. I also hoped to find a through line that would lend the story a satisfying shape and power. In the back of my mind, I knew it was extremely unlikely (impossible, actually) to fit all the scenes and locations into a nine-day schedule (eight days is the usual template, but the added day I was given hardly solved my problems). I owed it to the producers and to myself to calculate how much of what was written could be delivered within the time frame — to find the locations, determine how they might be grouped together efficiently, and develop my staging and visual strategies. Only after that could I recommend where trims, deletions, or (God forbid!) additions might be advisable. I knew that I had to fully immerse myself in the story and completely understand its subtext before I could make suggestions to help streamline the story to make it shootable.

In prep, location scouting is usually your first order of business. On day one, you'll board a scout van to visit "selects" of locations for the various scenes. As this process unfolds, the assistant director tries to group the sequences into a schedule that will make each day as efficient as possible. If most scenes fill only part of a shooting day, the AD will attempt to pair them with others in nearby locations so as to reduce move time. If you fall in love with a location for one sequence, the AD will try to find geographically compatible locations for scenes to be paired with it. It's a colossal and intricate puzzle with moving pieces, as "locked in" locations are sometimes lost at the last minute due to contract snags or because a rewrite renders a selected location no longer suitable.

My main focus at this early stage of prep is to find locations that appeal to me creatively, then assess how efficiently they might be shot. Where will the sun be at a particular time of day? How close to the set can we position the equipment trucks, and where can the crew park? How easy or difficult is it to control the activity of the neighborhood? What noise concerns are there? Once the assistant director and I process all that, in addition to considering the nature of the scene itself, we begin to get a sense of the time we'll need to complete a particular sequence.

During this part of the prep period, I'm generally in conversation with the showrunner, getting as much information as I can on each scene's point of view, its subtext, and the story points it needs to communicate. All of those questions will be more fully explored in the tone meeting, which is the director's chance to sit down with the writers and discuss these concerns in detail. That meeting often doesn't occur until later in the process, as rewrites may not have been completed. But scheduling needs to be set as soon as possible, so locations are often chosen with only partial information and may need to be rescouted or replaced once the script is finalized.

It all seems daunting, and truthfully, it frequently is. As many times as I've done this job, I still sometimes have sleepless nights (usually in mid-prep), anxiously pondering how on earth anyone could solve what feels like impossible production challenges. The fear of failure, if not complete humiliation, can arise with ferocity at any given time, but for me it's usually in the middle of the night. (Developing self-calming techniques, or a good meditation practice, is something I highly recommend.)

Among the many locations I needed to find for this episode of *Snowfall*, the opening stunt sequence generated the biggest challenge. It was very ambitious, but rich in defining what the season would be about. Andre, the beat cop whose daughter is the girlfriend of a drug dealer (the series' lead character), cruises the neighborhood in his police car. He notes how it has subtly changed since the show's previous season. More young men sport gold chains and are driving fancy cars — indications that the crack trade has taken hold. Andre (Marcus Henderson) sees a drug deal being transacted at a car stopped in the middle of the street. The car's driver negotiates with a young female crack addict who is leaning in through the car window. Andre parks and approaches. Seeing this, the dealer abruptly ends the negotiation, puts the car in gear, and tears off down the street. The crackhead, desperate for her fix, jumps into the accelerating vehicle, clawing for the drug, her body sticking halfway out of the speeding car's window, her legs flailing. The script indicated that Andre was to run back to his car and peel off in pursuit, stopping only after the woman — who has managed to grab some crack — flies off the dealer's car and falls onto the asphalt, unconscious. Andre races up to her and is shocked when she springs up with preternatural energy and takes off. She runs past a parked car, breaking off its radio antenna. With Andre in full pursuit, she stuffs the crack into the makeshift antenna pipe. We cut to Andre — still in pursuit, but now having lost her. As he turns to look around, he sees her crouched in a corner, exhaling smoke from the lit crack pipe, smiling dreamily and content for him to take her anywhere he'd like. The sequence ends with Andre's horrified recognition of how addictive this new drug is, and that it threatens to destroy the world he has known.

This is the audience's introduction to season three, and it needed to create immediate interest and impact. I wanted to open the scene by reminding the audience of past events and also pique interest about where we were picking up the story. The first season's pilot episode had a brilliant opening sequence — shot with an airborne drone — that featured the tall, graceful palm trees that line the streets of South Central's neighborhoods, presiding grandly over the lives of the residents below. I wanted the audience to recall that great shot, as well as be reminded of the more idyllic time of the first season. This would help set up the transformation we were going to dramatize. I also needed to find a tree-lined street that retained the architecture from the period, 1984.

We found two blocks that worked well; however, the opening sequence required a wider area if we were to shoot all of Andre's cruising as well as an exciting car chase. Even if we could find more blocks lined with palm trees close by, shooting at different locations would be costly in terms of move and set-up time. My solution was to shoot the same street several times, varying the angles to suggest different locations. This would give me more time to hone the performances and to shoot the necessary coverage.

My biggest concern for the opening sequence was the very dangerous car stunt. A high-speed chase with someone hanging on for dear life halfway outside the car is extremely dramatic precisely because it's life threatening. We needed to determine how to film this safely. In concert with the stunt coordinator, we devised a plan to anchor the stuntwoman from inside the car so that the wider shots from the street would make it appear as if she were in far more danger than she actually was. The cinematographer and I determined specific car mounts to give us exciting camera angles that would carry the audience along for the ride. I felt it was necessary to film the addict flying off the fast-moving car from both inside and outside the vehicle in order to create maximum visceral impact. But that meant I would need a stuntwoman who could also act. She needed to be convincing in this challenging part because it would be from her close-up angle that she would fall from the speeding car. We realized that if we also found a stuntman to play the dealer driving the car, we might create a real time-saver: Rather than having to tow the car from a camera vehicle — a great time-drain — we could rely on the stuntman to "free drive" and complete the sequence more quickly. I auditioned stuntmen and stuntwomen to see if we could find two who were skilled enough as actors. Happily, we did.

As this was only one time-consuming sequence in a script filled with others, we were simultaneously prepping all of them so that we could accurately assess where we stood in terms of the overall schedule. Only by quantifying how much time each ambitious sequence required could we know whether we would need to ask for extra days to be added to the schedule (not likely to be approved) or which scenes to suggest be eliminated. We soon realized that one major stunt event — the aerial sequence with the crash landing — would overtax our limited resources. While it added excitement to a marginally important story beat, it would have compromised our ability to give enough weight to the opening stunt sequence, which was vital to the show's thematic concerns. Again, always think story.

Even with that savings, it was apparent we would have to complete the opening sequence in just one day if we were not to shortchange all the other critically important scenes. I couldn't yet figure out a way to do that, especially since we were shooting in early winter when the days are shortest. I could only count on roughly nine hours of daylight, during which, at some point, we would have to break for lunch. I had done all I could to come up with a smart staging plan, a way to employ three cameras for most shots, and an order of shooting that would take advantage of where the sun was located at any given time. But we were still trying to fit the proverbial ten pounds into a five-pound bag.

A director's will and imagination really get tested when confronting the reality that the original draft of a script is too ambitious. It's one thing to acknowledge what cannot be done. But that doesn't necessarily mean you have to resign yourself to doing something less good. By staying committed to the story you're telling, you may surprise yourself and your collaborators by making a virtue out of limitation. If you cannot simply throw money at the problem, how might the story otherwise be told? I have found that ingenuity is more likely to occur when your attention is fixed on the essentials of the story you're telling.

I heard an account (maybe apocryphal) of something Francis Coppola came up with on *The Godfather Part II*. He was over budget and couldn't afford to build the set of young Vito's room on Ellis

Island anywhere near the Statue of Liberty, which he wanted as a poignant reminder of the aspirational dreams of immigrants to this country. Denied the resources to shoot the sequence the way he imagined it, he came up with the idea of what has become an iconic shot: the face of the boy staring out his window next to a reflection in the glass of what was actually a photograph of the Statue of Liberty. This solution imbued the image with more visual poetry than the expensive alternative likely would have, and it sprang from a limitation Coppola had to accept, as well as from attention to what was essential about the scene.

I had been keeping the showrunner/writer (Dave Andron) advised of my progress on the opening scene, informing him that the number of shots required to cover all the story beats within the action was very problematic. I had begun to realize that the bridge too far was Andre's lengthy foot pursuit that came after the car chase. Filming this involved not just moving to backyards and alleyways, but also shooting several detailed insert shots to show the breaking off of the antenna and packing the crack into the makeshift pipe, all while moving at speed. Then there was the problem of justifying how a physically fit police officer could trail so far behind the fleeing woman that she'd have time enough to lose him, light her crack pipe, and surprise the audience as well. Dave explained that the reason for the extended sequence was to show the extreme lengths to which a crack addict would go to get a fix, impressing upon Andre that this was unlike any drug he'd ever encountered.

I suggested a slight change in the chase sequence that would solve the logical problem of Andre not being able to keep up with the addict. First, if, rather than heading back to his own car to pursue the fleeing dealer, Andre took off running to chase after him, he could be winded when he pulls up to check on the condition of the fallen woman. This would justify why he couldn't follow her at full speed when she takes off. It also would help in foreshortening the length of the pursuit to simply one block, fitting more easily into our one location.

But then I started to reflect on the purpose of the sequence, as described by the writer. What seemed most important was that Andre sees that this drug leads to fanatical and desperate efforts to stay high, at the expense of all other concerns: Pain and jeopardy were irrelevant to those addicted to crack. The scene as written seemed to have two endings: the first when the woman rolled to a stop on the pavement; the second after she had run off and gotten high. It was the second ending that was making the scene unmakeable within our time frame. How might we raise the stakes at the first stop to hit all the notes important to the writer *and* avoid the trouble of filming another extended chase? I pitched to the writer that the addict could already have a crack pipe on her. That way we could cut down the time-consuming subsequent chase. Then, if the fall from the car looked gnarly enough, Andre would arrive expecting to find her critically injured, only to see her turn toward him, exhaling smoke from a lit crack pipe and staring at him blissfully, oblivious to what must be searing pain. That alone might trigger in him (and the audience) all the writer hoped to convey.

With some regret, Dave agreed to let go of the extended chase. We at least now had a fighting chance to complete the sequence in one day. I did a detailed shot list and also created, with my DP and assistant director, an efficient order to shoot each setup so as to get the most efficient lighting conditions possible. The shooting order depended on "chasing the backlight": shooting into wherever the sun was positioned and being less dependent on creating backlight artificially. We did all the proper prep, which included procuring two identical cars for the drug dealer. This allowed us to affix our stabilizing camera mounts and lighting equipment on the vehicle we'd be using for interior shots while keeping the car we'd be seeing from the street free of any camera and grip mounts attached to it. We would thereby reduce the downtime between setups by quickly switching from filming one car to the other, each ready at all times.

Still, when I arrived on the day of the shoot, my assistant director told me that he had timed the shot list and figured we would get through only about two-thirds of my shots by the time the sun set. Concerned but not convinced, I kept to the plan, consolidated shots where possible, moved on when I had the footage I needed, and probably barked a little more than usual that everyone continue to work quickly and to anticipate what would be needed for the next shot. We continued to beat all the timing estimates and looked to be in good shape to get everything we needed. But I also knew, and kept reminding myself, "You can't ever let up."

No matter how well-prepared and shot-listed you may be, your ability to remain flexible in the moment — to adjust your plan and stay open to what you haven't anticipated — is a significant skill to cultivate. You must stay closely attentive to what is going on right in front of you in case something happens that makes your well-conceived plans obsolete. Sometimes we can't control which way the ball bounces or, in the case of this sequence, which way the body rolls on the pavement.

I was especially concerned about the stuntwoman's safety when she would have to throw herself from the speeding car. The rewrite now had her rolling across the pavement and landing halfway behind a parked car so that, as Andre runs toward her, he sees only her legs sticking out past the car's rear wheel. When he finally arrives, she would be turning toward him and exhaling from the crack pipe. In this way, I felt, the viewer would fear she was dead or unconscious, and then discover that she had used the time hidden behind the car to fill and light her pipe. The whole design of the sequence depended on our stuntwoman landing in the correct position. If she didn't, we could likely create the impression that she had by "match-cutting" to a tight shot of her landing where I wanted her to be.

To achieve this, the stuntwoman would need to propel herself off the moving car — slowed down as much as possible, but still credibly fast — and skid across the pavement into a dead-drop stop. To help create the sense of a violent roll, I "under-cranked" the camera to make both her and the car's movements appear faster. From outside the moving vehicle, the dismount itself looked slightly artificial, since she had to create the spring necessary to hurl herself toward the curb. It looked almost like a jump, which it wasn't supposed to be. That was why I wanted the shot from inside the car; with it, we would be able to see the stuntwoman in her close-up simply drop away from the window and onto an off-camera platform attached to the moving car. This would enable me to cut out the false-looking moment in the exterior shot when she initiates her jump. Stitched together, the two pieces of film created a perception of the rag-doll effect I wanted and the sense that the car itself had propelled the woman along a violent and lengthy roll to a stop. It was a dangerous stunt, and even though the stuntwoman wore pads, bouncing across the street could not have felt good. We did a first take, which simply didn't work, then a second one, which was great in all regards except one: She hadn't come to a stop anywhere near the rear of the parked car. Even a tighter insert shot of her landing at the appropriate spot would have created a poorly edited sequence and strain credibility that she had in fact landed there.

I was concerned for the stuntwoman, preferring not to have her do it again. She had sold the hard fall beautifully, which I knew was courageous and undoubtedly painful. Many injuries occur on unnecessary extra takes of stunts, so I felt it only right to move on. But how could I incorporate this new body position into the sequence I had designed? I saw that at least she had landed facing away from Andre as he ran up behind her, and she could still turn in position to reveal the lit crack pipe. With the sun getting lower, I chose to move on.

We continued shooting the other coverage as planned. I hoped that with skillful editing, it would be plausible that Andre could believe the addict was out cold. We started from where the woman had landed to see Andre fast approaching. Before moving the camera to film Andre's point of view, I completed a shot in which the Steadicam moved past the addict's inert body to meet Andre running toward her and the camera. This momentarily held the two actors in the same frame, tying them together. I told the stunt-woman to lie still until after the camera had passed so as not to tip that she was in any way conscious. Then I reversed angles, running behind Andre as he approached the woman, and cued her to turn toward him when he was almost upon her. In the first take, she thought she had heard my signal and started her motion significantly too early, while Andre was fairly far away. We did it again, and she waited until exactly the moment I wanted.

Later that night, mentally reviewing the day's work, I bolted up in bed, understanding that I had made a potentially disastrous error: If the woman was visibly unconscious until right before she turns to Andre, how on earth would she have been able to load the crack pipe and light it, yet still appear (even from behind) to be flat on the ground, out cold? All of my shots had been carefully designed not to tip her loading the pipe so it would be a shock when Andre arrived by her side. This hadn't been a problem with the original plan because her upper torso would have been shielded from view; it was credible that she would have been able to load and light the pipe while keeping her lower body still.

I knew I could probably edit the scene in a way to get around the problem, but it would involve eliminating all of the tie-in shots in which we see both characters in the same frame. The energetic Steadicam shots — one over the woman's body, the other behind Andre running toward her — would likely be truncated, creating a far inferior sequence. Then I remembered the blown take, the first one, in which the stuntwoman had started her action much earlier than I had wanted.

It was as if a life raft had materialized to rescue my drowning hopes. I saw that I could now establish her making some faint movement as Andre approached. That would be all I'd need to bring the audience fully along and not question how the woman had gotten the crack pipe ready and lit. I also found that Andre's reaction was more than strong enough to hit all the story points we needed in the moment. I had been saved by an error, by something I had not planned, but which I had been fortunate to remember and could insert into a new editing pattern. This would slightly alter the events, but it saved a dynamic sequence from being visually diminished. It was good luck, and I was grateful for it.

Toward the end of the long day, we raced to get the shot that had originally brought me to this location: the establishing shot for opening *Snowfall's* season, meant to evoke the world of the show. I felt we were in good shape timewise as the camera and grip departments mounted a "remote head" on the top of Andre's police car. A remote head is a camera operated away from the device itself, enabling it to be placed in tight or inaccessible quarters. After considering a drone shot to mimic the one I admired from pilot, I rejected the idea, wanting to be more connected to the character of Andre. Remember: The story point was the new understanding Andre was going to have after his experience with the crazed drug addict. In fact, this was going to set him up as the crusading adversary of the show's anti-hero drug dealer, his daughter's boyfriend. In all the hubbub of getting through the day's work, it was vital not to lose sight of the scene's raison d'être: to define and kick off the season we were introducing. Instead of coming in from a point of view above the world, I opted to tilt down from the towering palms to reveal the light bar atop Andre's police car as it cruises through the neighborhood. The scene is Andre's; I wanted to be in his viewpoint. Although this shot wasn't strictly his POV, it would naturally transition to it once we cut to the second camera that was shooting simultaneously from the passenger seat and looking out the front windshield. This would firmly put the viewers in Andre's mind and experience.

The staging was complex. Tilting down from the swaying palm trees gliding past the traveling car, the camera, anchored to the car's roof, settled at eye level to reveal the busy street life. An extra would cross in front of a flashy convertible driving past Andre's police car, motivating the second camera to pan left with the convertible to reveal Andre in profile. These would be the first images viewers would have of the third season.

Timing was critical, and it began to seem that all the elements might not come together before the sun dipped too low. I sat in the police car's back seat with the camera operator and a hand-held monitor to see the image. On our third try, and right before the sun would be past its ideal position, we started forward with the camera pointing up to see the trees glide past the frame. It seemed to me impossibly long — too long — before the operator began the camera's tilt down to the street, which I knew would be critical to time exactly. I called out, "Background action!" to start things at what I guessed would be the correct time. To my great astonishment and relief, this last chance at the shot turned out perfectly. It was beautiful, almost elegiac. I knew then that we had accomplished what had once seemed impossible: We had all the shots and performances we would need to make a fantastic introductory sequence.

We finished just as the sun dipped below the horizon. We then moved to our nighttime location, which we had tacked on to fill out the twelve hours of shooting time we were budgeted for. I felt greatly relieved, creatively fulfilled, and full of appreciation for the cast and crew, who had come together to pull off a pretty remarkable achievement. And this was just one of nine jam-packed days, each of which required us to work diligently to wring all we possibly could from conditions limited by production restrictions that, in truth, are always part of the job.

It's a wonderful feeling, when you're committed to telling a great story, to find the depth of each character and moment, and to see opportunities where others might experience only limitations. This was an example of making a difficult stunt sequence work under trying circumstances. But the same challenge can apply to any sort of scene, as, for example, when an actor is struggling to nail a difficult performance. If you find, as can often be the case, that the company is drifting into overtime and there is pressure to complete the work in a timely fashion, remind yourself that you're never again going to "step into this river." Never again will you have the opportunity to make *this* moment true for *this* character in *this* story. Sometimes, that sort of hyperfocus can lead to an inspired note or pull from you resources you didn't know you possessed. Remember, this is a special opportunity. Only *you* determine when it's time to say, "Good enough." And that is a bar one ought to set high: Making an ambitious show makeable does not have to mean making it less good.

CHAPTER ELEVEN

TAKING RISKS: *MANHATTAN*

A N IMPORTANT MEASURE OF SERIES TELEVISION DIRECTORS is how much of a script's full potential they have managed to realize in the finished product. How successful were they at finding meanings, subtleties, and compelling visuals to give the viewer a truly immersive storytelling experience? The first order of business, of course, is delivering a completed show, with a coherent beginning, middle, and end. But how deeply you explore the story and how you translate it into a makeable schedule — even when a wrench is thrown into your best-laid plans — is what separates one director from the next. The ability to assess a changing situation and adjust appropriately, knowing when to take a risk, is an essential skill for an episodic director to cultivate.

Manhattan was a show that aired on the WGN network for two seasons. It was a series that unfortunately did not get the attention it deserved in the current intense competition for viewership. It dealt with the race between the Nazis and the Allied Forces to develop the atomic bomb during World War II. The U.S. government brought the most brilliant scientists from all over the country to Los Alamos, New Mexico, to try to create a nuclear device before the Nazis could. The show's first season focused on the progress of two distinct teams of scientists, each pursuing a different theory of how to produce the bomb. The enmity between the two leaders of each team threatened to derail the whole enterprise.

I directed an episode, "The Gun Model," that picked up the story at the point when one of the team leaders, Reed Akely (David Harbour), is currently the favorite of the officials who determine which approach will be funded. His junior scientist, Charlie Isaacs (Ashley Zukerman), suspects that Akely's personal ambition has led him to conceal problematic research results, thus skewing the evaluation process in his team's favor. As a result, resources have been diverted from the rival team. With the stakes so high, Isaacs steals classified data so that the other team can do an independent evaluation of it; all the while, he pretends to Akely that he suspects nothing.

The script included a two-character, four-and-a-half-page sequence that occurs after Akely discovers Isaacs has betrayed him. This sequence starts with Akely's car pulling to a stop on a remote desert road. Akely and Isaacs exit the car and head off into the desert. Akely carries a shotgun, ostensibly to hunt wildlife. After a few hundred yards, he stops and angrily confronts Isaacs about his betrayal, firing his shotgun into the desert air as he struggles to contain his outrage. Aware that Akely might be threatening to shoot him right there, Isaacs bravely reveals that he knows all about Akely's misrepresentations and doctored lab work; this is what had motivated him to try to set things right. Akely unexpectedly softens, seeming finally to understand how his young associate could have gotten things so wrong. He shares with Isaacs previously undisclosed classified information that, if true, would fully exonerate him and prove that his team's version of the bomb is certain to work. As Isaacs realizes in horror that he'd misjudged the situation, Akely goes on to suggest that Isaacs has been used by the rival scientist, who had taken advantage of his naïveté and inexperience. Worse than that, the other team leader has gotten him to steal classified documents, which could expose Isaacs to a charge of treason and a likely firing squad.

Isaacs is now desperate and looks helplessly at Akely, who seems finally in control of his outrage. Assuming a fatherly demeanor, Akely puts his arm around the young scientist and agrees to give him another chance. Isaacs is left with a deep sense of gratitude, and fury at the other team leader's cynical and self-serving agenda.

Great scene, brilliantly written, involving characters challenged to the core of their being undergoing subtle, moment-to-moment shifts in their thoughts and emotions. I was very excited to direct it. But what made this so difficult to accomplish was that it all took place at the first light of dawn.

A sequence of this complexity would normally require extensive rehearsal and then several takes of each angle just to get the acting beats right. Plus, it covered a wide expanse of terrain, requiring equipment to be set, moved, and reset to adequately cover the action. Even if there were no location or daylight concerns, this sequence might easily take half a day or more to complete. But it was all supposed to take place at dawn. The only way I knew to suspend the sun just below the horizon was via green screen and computer-graphic imagery, which far exceeded our resources to pull off.

Usually, when a production team is presented with this sort of challenge, it will ask for a rewrite to change the sequence to either an all-day or an all-night scene. This eliminates the problems caused by quickly changing light conditions. Scenes far less complicated than this one are nearly always rewritten to avoid that very issue. Yet I wanted to deliver the scene as scripted. The New Mexico desert is spectacular in low light. But more germane to the storytelling was that the events being dramatized in this high-stakes series dealt with the darkest possibilities imaginable: unleashing the nuclear genie or failing to stop Hitler. Plus, this episode would have a shocking surprise at its conclusion: Akely would be exposed as having in fact withheld crucial information to keep his project afloat, jeopardizing the entire war effort. He will be revealed as having doctored his research and lying to Isaacs because of his own terror at admitting failure. And he will kill himself at the end of the episode.

Not much in the episodes leading up to this point had laid the groundwork for Akely being suicidal. David Harbour had given his character a solid presence, likeable and aboveboard. The audience had always seen him behave positively and responsibly. I felt I needed to introduce a dark side to his character that would later be understood as the beginning of his final descent. I'm sure the writers felt the same way in conceiving the sequence as a night journey leading to what turns out to be a false dawn. By keeping the heated exchange in murky light, there would be a visceral association that each of the characters is in a terribly dark place internally. The dawning light metaphorically supports a dramatic misdirect — certainly for Isaacs — that a new, truer light is emerging, taking suspicion off of Akely and also contributing to the sense of a new day. It would position the audience to be in precisely the subjective state best suited to involve them in the story, suggesting at first a sort of "dark night of the soul" for each of the characters, and then the feeling of enlightenment growing out of what I hoped the viewer would experience as an honest reckoning between the two men.

There were other scenes to be shot in desert locations, requiring the production team to go through the usual drill of estimating how much time would be required for each one. In total, we would need two full days in the desert to complete this scene, together with all the other work. We knew the quality of light appropriate for the dawn scene would last, at tops, an hour and a half. This estimate allowed for post-production corrections that could be made in the "color timing," which can make an image look slightly brighter or darker than what is originally photographed. An hour and a half, however, was not enough time to film a four-and-a-half-page sequence, let alone one with characters moving significant distances — and all to be shot at "first light." We considered dividing the work over the two days we would be shooting in the desert, but I was uneasy committing to a plan that relied on the weather matching from one day to the next. Rain was always a possibility, and the New Mexico sky could vary greatly in appearance. Also, breaking up the performance for the actors on so demanding a scene was in itself counterproductive to getting their best work.

A lengthy rehearsal to nail down the staging and the beats of the performance would be absolutely necessary for this emotionally complicated scene. One timesaver would be to rehearse the actors and set the camera positions before the light was right for us to shoot. That pointed me to an opportunity, which led to the creation of our plan. The sun just below the horizon looks the same whether it's rising or setting, so we decided to shoot the scene at sunset instead of the literal dawn, which the audience would never realize. We would shoot our other day scenes nearby so that I could rehearse with David and Ashley during set-up times for those other scenes. Then, because the more the sun sank below the horizon, the "earlier" the light would appear in the story, we would shoot the sequence in reverse order from how it would be edited together. Because most of the key acting moments take place after the actors finish their walk and confront each other directly, we could maximize the time available to perfect those key moments and be in a better position to gauge when we'd need to move to film the car's arrival in near darkness. This could be handled in wide shots, simpler to shoot and less performance-dependent. If any snags occurred, it would be better to hurry the arrival than the dramatic heart of the scene. It would all be a rush, of course, but story takes priority.

I asked for one more thing that would be crucial to complete the scene on time. Most directors of photography are averse to something called "cross shooting." The term describes using two cameras to shoot opposite directions simultaneously. Cross shooting makes it more difficult to "sculpt" the light, which has to appear the same, even though it's shot from two distinct directions. But with a strong enough sidelight on each of the two actors (accomplished by placing them both in profile to the sun, shining on the sides of their faces farthest from the camera), some cameramen can make this work. I knew our only chance to get the scene in our limited time frame was to shoot both sides of the coverage simultaneously in each lens size. This would ensure that their actions "matched" (the actors' physical actions would always be in sync with one another because they would be happening at once on both sides of the coverage) and probably require fewer takes. Our talented cameraman, Richard Rutkowski, was excited by the challenge.

Now we had a plan I felt pretty good about. I would rehearse the scene fully, making sure to stage all the actors' movements so that each camera could avoid seeing the other covering its subject. The quickest way to film would be handheld so that each camera operator would have the freedom to move however he'd need to cover considerable distances and also be able to ad lib his positioning in case the actors moved in unrehearsed ways. My priority was the raw truthfulness of the performances, and I didn't want the actors second-guessing themselves about following an authentic impulse that might not have been rehearsed. The operators knew it was their job to adjust in the moment. Fortuitously, this camera style gave the sequence an edgy, less stable energy that might connote danger as well as uncertainty as to where events might lead.

Richard and I thought it would be wise to order a third camera and crew so that we could sneak in an additional angle where possible, giving us more flexibility in the editing room. Richard also thought the extra camera would save us some time if our wider "scope" shot could be set up while we finished filming our tighter coverage. Any advantage we could eke out to beat the setting sun was well worth the expense.

The day arrived for shooting, and the other daylight scenes went off without a hitch. I was able to get in enough rehearsal time to work out all of the staging and beats of the scene. We rehearsed both the main confrontation and also the car's arrival at the road a few hundred yards away. The plan was to end with the arrival, since it was the introduction to the scene and needed to look the darkest (or "earliest"). We found ourselves fully rehearsed, with cameras set, while we waited for the sun to drop low enough for us to begin filming. It was around 5:45p.m., still too light to feel like dawn. So we decided to wait until 6:30 to start our sprint toward 8p.m., when it would feel like true night and we could no longer shoot. I knew we would be rushed, but I felt confident the actors would nail each setup in one or two takes. I was particularly pleased that there were beautiful clouds in the sky, promising a spectacular sunset with a pink and golden glow.

While we waited, the clouds continued to gather. Then they darkened, creating a tremendously dramatic backdrop hovering over a band of golden light on the horizon. At around 6:20, the assistant director summoned the actors and crew to assemble and get ready to start filming.

Then lightning struck.

Not right on top of us, but near enough that the whole spectacular valley was illuminated. My first worry was rain, but that didn't seem to be coming. Then I noticed the crew heading back to the trucks and remembered a safety rule that all shooting companies must observe: No crew can be asked to work on an exterior set until thirty minutes have passed since the last lightning strike in the area. I felt sick. After all the lengths to which we had gone to try to pull off this sequence, after all the prep, it appeared now to be for naught. Shooting the scene in an hour and a half would be difficult at best. Anything significantly less than that looked to be impossible. I huddled with the DP and the AD, but there wasn't much we could do. I was just hoping no further lightning would strike so the thirty-minute clock wouldn't have to restart. As the minutes ticked away, I stared at the truck caravan where the crew was seeking shelter, desperately hoping to see them emerge and head my way.

The sky was turning more brilliant in color as the sun dropped lower, and I thought how beautiful the shots would have been had we been able to film then. How much longer would the horizon appear so dazzling? A producer happened to be on set, and I asked how things might be reconceived to shorten the sequence. Perhaps the actors didn't need to be shown arriving in their car and could instead be introduced in a wide shot as they marched across the desert? I was hoping to cut the arrival so I wouldn't have to rush the performances even more than I would already be forced to do. Assuming we would be able to start shooting at all, it seemed critical that we not jeopardize getting the best possible performances just to establish that the characters had driven a car to get there. But he was reluctant to give up anything. I knew that if it came to it, I would shoot the confrontation until I had gotten the performances I wanted, sacrificing the arrival. But I was hoping I wouldn't have to.

At 7:25p.m., the crew emerged from the trucks, satisfied that the required time had elapsed so that shooting could begin. Okay, game on. I wasn't sure how much we would get on film, and I knew that I would likely not get all the coverage angles I'd hoped for. The actors jumped into position and, of course, we started rolling right away.

I've often noticed on film sets that the passage of time can seem to vary wildly. I don't propose a mystical explanation for it, and it certainly doesn't always occur, but there are times — particularly when the company is significantly behind schedule, and everyone is filled with the urgency to work quickly and efficiently — that time seems to slow down. Maybe it's owing to a kind of hyper-focus, but it's an amazing feeling to complete a camera setup, check your watch, and then discover that much less time has passed than you would have guessed. Fortunately, this turned out to be one of those times.

David and Ashley were in the zone and delivered beautiful, close-up, line-perfect performances. My eyes darted between the monitors to see if both cameras had captured the important moments. Having a good one "in the can," I backed up the cameras slightly to make room for the third camera, and I captured a tight two-shot for the moment when Akely puts his arm around Isaacs, forgiving him in a fatherly way. The gesture recalled an already established longing that Isaacs had for his own absent father. Seeing how quickly we had gotten these angles, I went for wider overs, shooting full-body shots of each character while holding the other in the foreground. This would give the audience a chance to breathe and sense the surrounding environment in between experiencing the more intense, tighter coverage shots. The glow from the setting sun still peeked above the horizon, and I dropped back to get a vista shot of the characters walking into position. We were ready to race to the road to see if we might still have time to shoot the car arriving. But Richard surprised me with the third camera having already moved back to grab a wider shot still, which was glorious and provided a magnificent frame to end the sequence on the two men, small figures against the brilliant colors of the desert sky. I couldn't say no, even if it meant there would be no time to shoot the arrival.

When we got to the road, it looked to me that there might not be enough light to shoot. But Richard assured me that he could time the shot in post-production so it would look brighter than how it appeared to our eyes. Also, I knew that because we had shot the sequence in reverse, it wouldn't really matter if it was quite dark because that part of the scene occurs earliest in the sequence. Again, the two cameras hurried into position, and we simultaneously shot both a wide and a tighter frame of the car driving up, then the actors exiting it and moving off into the desert. It was 8:11p.m. We had shot the entire four-and-a-half pages in forty-six minutes. And I was certain it would be one of the most photographically beautiful sequences I had ever filmed. More importantly, it delivered a powerful dramatic moment.

I would have been extremely pleased if we had been able to finish the scene in the hour and a half we thought nearly impossible. But I was ecstatic to have emerged with so excellent a version in much shorter time. We had almost literally caught lightning in a bottle.

It doesn't always work out so well. There's nearly always a plan B, of course, for those times when adversity can't be overcome. In this case, it would have meant returning to the location on another day, at considerable cost, and figuring out a simpler way to complete the work — probably making it a daytime scene. But it turned out to be well worth the challenge, and I was thrilled that it had paid off. The natural elements enhanced the story and deepened the audience's experience of the characters' inner lives. It took detailed planning, a huge collaborative effort, and a little luck — after, of course, some bad luck. But being able to adjust when unexpected events occur — figuring out other ways to solve a problem — is a key job requirement for series directors, as is, at times, being willing to roll the dice. All that will be remembered is what ends up on the screen.

CHAPTER TWELVE

FINDING THE BIGGER PICTURE: *GOOD GIRLS REVOLT*

S OMETIMES YOU'LL READ A SCRIPT AND RECOGNIZE a scene that contains effective dramatic moments but just doesn't seem to connect with the show's larger concerns. Of course, not every scene *can* do that. Some scenes are needed simply to move along the narrative. But it's always important to honor any intuition that tells you there is something more to explore.

That was the sense I had when I was directing an episode of a show set during a fascinating period in the history of the women's rights movement. *Good Girls Revolt*, on Amazon, was a period drama that took its inspiration from a class-action lawsuit brought by the female employees of *Newsweek* magazine in the early 1970s. Discrimination against women was so pervasive that it was an official policy in many places, including large corporations. At the time, *Newsweek* required all its published articles to be credited to men, even though women worked as research partners to male reporters and often co-wrote the stories. With few exceptions, no women were ever officially recognized as having contributed to articles published in the magazine. Management operated under the belief that a man's name signaled authority and clear thinking. It's strange to consider how recently in our history this practice was considered sane, fair, or intelligent. Discrimination took an additional toll on women, as they also faced inner conflicts about asserting themselves, their confidence shaken by a lack of institutional support.

This was not only a historically significant story to tell; it also promised meaningful inner journeys for its characters, who were challenged to summon the courage to confront injustice and claim their rights in the workplace. In my episode, entitled "Out of Pocket," one of the researchers, Patti, is a social activist who passionately opposes racial oppression. She convinces Doug, the male reporter for whom she works at the show's fictional magazine (*News of the Week*) to write a story about the slaying of three Black Panthers (a Black-empowerment organization in the '60s) during a police raid of the victims' home. The violent confrontation also resulted in the death of a police officer, but Patti feels the police themselves were responsible for that death. In her view, the police were functioning as an arm of the white power structure brutalizing Black people. Doug, who is also Patti's lover, has benefited from her journalistic instincts as he has moved up the ladder at the magazine. But he is more inclined to treat the story in what he regards as an evenhanded way, wanting to focus in equal parts on the tragedy of the white police officer's death and the deaths of the Black victims. As he is the one whose byline will be on the article, he has final say.

In a scene that takes place in a bar where Patti and Doug go after the funeral for the slain officer, we see that each has been affected by the service in very different ways; Doug has responded to the communal solidarity fellow officers have provided to the grieving family, who take pride in their loved one for his sacrifice; Patti, on the other hand, focuses on comments she overheard about "the neighborhood changing" and the "better past," which she feels carry the subtext: *before integration*. She is upset at the implied racism.

The two journalists share their thoughts and observations. Patti expresses outrage at the racist attitudes she's just witnessed and believes the good-old-boys network of white cops is responsible for a possibly unconstitutional raid on the Black household. Doug feels the poignance of the white family's loss and questions the implications Patti has read into the eulogies. He simply isn't interested in writing a politically tinged polemic and wants to focus on the tragedy visited on all the families. Patti is nearly beside herself as she passionately argues her position, pointing out what she sees as a false equivalency. She persists in advocating for what she believes is the real story: the racist abuse of power. He grows weary of her repeating the same arguments and exits the bar.

As scenes go, this one certainly had drama. But I felt the experience needed to be understood in a greater context than Patti's frustration at what she takes to be Doug's infuriating naïveté, or even that racism is a terrible problem in our society. The bigger context as it related to this story — and what I wanted the scene to further — was that women were beginning to realize that they could no longer tolerate simply being cheerleaders and support personnel for their male counterparts. Their growing frustration was a necessary precondition for the rise of the women's rights movement. It could be argued that the scene as written conveyed some of this frustration in an indirect way by virtue of Patti's urgent desire to have her values represented in the article. But something felt to me like a missed opportunity.

In prep, I asked the writers about this scene, focusing on the last beat when Doug exits, leaving Patti alone at the bar. It seemed to me that this was where we might link the scene to the more significant overall story. We felt Patti's frustration, but nothing more. I suggested adding a line at the end of the scripted dialogue, which might give me the hook I needed to land the moment in a more cogent way. If Doug were to say, as he excused himself, "I have to write it the way I see it," it might point us to the deeper themes because that was precisely what the women themselves were thirsting for the chance to do. The showrunner agreed and added the line.

I was scheduled to shoot the bar scene on what's known as a second-unit day: The main unit had already moved on to the next episode. As I had only the one scene left to shoot, I was given a reduced crew to film on a different soundstage, away from where the first (or main) unit was shooting. We would get the actress playing Patti (Genevieve Angelson) only after the first unit had completed its work with her.

As sometimes happens, the first unit encountered delays and fell behind its original time estimates. In order for Genevieve to complete her scenes in the next episode, she had worked the entire morning and early afternoon, missing her lunch break, and as a result was suffering from low blood sugar. She hurried to join our second unit, exhausted and barely able to generate the energy required for the heightened emotional demands of the bar scene. When we started shooting, Genevieve did all she could to generate indignation at the racism her character had just witnessed. Her emotion spilled over into outrage at her partner for not agreeing with her. The actor playing Doug (Hunter Parrish) tried to meet her passion with understanding, while still holding on to his belief that he saw the story in perhaps a more nuanced way. This further inflamed Genevieve (as Patti), who threw her hands up, appearing almost as an avenging angel. Her angry condemnation grew to such a pitch that, when Doug left the bar, it felt like this would be the end of their relationship.

On the one hand, I was glad Genevieve had succeeded in investing emotionally in the scene, fatigued as she was. She had connected to the story. But I hadn't envisioned her character becoming quite so incensed, overwhelming her partner with outrage. It could be justified, certainly, if this were a moment when Patti's passion for social justice was the thing to explore; there were plenty of circumstances to point us to that conclusion: Genevieve's character was a child of the '60s, outraged by racial inequality; she had just witnessed what she took to be self-justifying racist attitudes. But my feeling was that the emotional choice overwhelmed the moment, forced her scene partner into a purely defensive reaction, and offered no resolution other than the sense that these two coworkers and lovers were finished with each other.

Something key was missing. I felt I had lost track of the larger story. Now was the time, if ever there would be, to figure out what the answer was to the question that had gnawed at me from the start: What was missing? And again, it started with a detail. Genevieve's anger had resulted in her being cut off from her scene partner. Why did that feel wrong to me? I thought of the line that had been added at the end of the scene, the way it mirrored what the women wanted for themselves: to write things the way *they* saw them. It seemed at first not directly applicable to Patti's situation, since she wasn't being allowed to write at all. But if she were to win that right, it would only have meaning if she could truly express her honest viewpoints. What opened up for me was a different way of imagining the scene and the intention with which Patti enters it. Genevieve had accessed the first layer of what underpins her character: Patti's core value of standing up for justice, which was what motivated her to become a journalist in the first place. The passion Genevieve gave vent to had enabled her to inhabit the character, which I appreciated because the actress's physical condition of fatigue had made that challenging. But if the scene stayed at that pitch and level of self-righteousness, it lost my interest. What was it I wanted to see? I was interested in how this scene could advance the larger story we were telling. When I registered that the actress's choice had led to a cutoff from her scene partner, I found the detail that pointed me to an alternative choice and a richer meaning.

I took her aside and suggested a new approach to the scene: The reason Patti is arguing so vehemently is that she has no voice herself and must depend on Doug to articulate her point of view. The tone and tenor of what she tells him mustn't be quite so strident because her only hope is to bring him to her side, to convince him that hers is the more important story to tell. He is Patti's only hope for conveying her point of view to the magazine's readers. If she vilifies him, she will drive him into defensiveness and make him less likely to embrace her way of thinking. She should try other strategies, even if they are to cajole or gently persuade. She might reach a point of anger and frustration, but if she does, she'll need to become aware that she is failing to convince him, which might well lead to redoubling her efforts to suppress her anger, so strong is her intention to get her view expressed.

Genevieve became intrigued, and I continued: "When he gets up to leave, saying only 'I have to write it the way I see it,' that doesn't signal the scene is over. It's actually the key moment when something more important comes into focus for you — more important than whatever version of the story gets written. You see in him the embodiment of exactly what you deserve for yourself: the right to express yourself truthfully and without having to please others. The problem is that *he* gets to write his point of view and that *you* don't. He's not the enemy. The system in place at *News of the Week* is the enemy because it has completely disempowered you. You've been trying to twist Doug into a version of yourself to get your views expressed. As he walks off and delivers his last line, I'd like to see you let go of advocating for your version of events and be with this deeper insight that it's not Doug's job to stand up for your voice. It's yours."

In that moment, the actress shed all her fatigue, became suffused with excitement, and delivered a pitch-perfect performance. She brought new levels of insight to the moment and accessed a part of herself that was deeper, and more fully human. The scene now reflected what the entire series was about. Perhaps more importantly, watching her go through the process of awakening permitted the audience to better identify with her character, making them more emotionally invested in the story going forward.

This is your job as the director: not to rest until you have exhausted every opportunity to improve the story. It would have felt natural and realistic to play the scene as simply being about two people with strong points of view arguing for their values. But that would have done little to shine light on a more interesting dilemma the character of Patti was facing: having something to say with no way or platform to say it. That is exactly the tension that drives the larger story: the emergence of consciousness. It's far better, almost always, to watch characters undergo transformation as it happens to them than to be presented with the before and after versions of themselves. The reimagining of this scene afforded us the chance to watch Patti's consciousness emerge in the moment, enriching the experience and clarifying the meaning of her story.

This is another example of the importance of honoring the questions that arise within you. A perceptive audience will be asking intuitively the same ones: How does this make me feel? What feels deficient about this moment in terms of the overall story? Why isn't it landing with my sense of what this moment should be? Only by asking the questions do you invite your inner resources to come up with answers. Part of this process is searching for ways to connect story elements that feel isolated from one another. Look for ways they may be associated, and work to see what hidden connections can advance the main story.

Don't settle, or at least don't settle too soon. When confronted with an obstacle or a limitation — like the unfairness of a schedule that hands you an exhausted actress for an important scene — don't rationalize that it's okay for your product to be less good because of it. Work hard to push through the limitation. You'll sometimes confront having to shoot a scene more simply than you'd planned because delays have shortened the amount of time you have to complete it. If your commitment to the storytelling is focused enough, you may come up with a more economical way of shooting that proves more effective than your original idea. Resist, as best you can, feeling like a victim of circumstances or lamenting the situation to the point that you forget: This is your one chance to land *this* moment in a story that you likely will never be telling again.

CHAPTER THIRTEEN

WORKING WITH THE SHOWRUNNER

P ROBABLY THE BIGGEST DIFFERENCE BETWEEN DIRECTING AN episode of television and directing a feature film is the primary role that showrunners play in the world of series television. The showrunner is often the writer and creator of the show. They guide the writing process, communicate with the network or streaming service, and generally have final say on most creative decisions. It's not uncommon for department heads to run a director's choices past the showrunner for final approval. These include casting preferences, location selections, production design, wardrobe, and hairstyles. If there is disagreement, it's usually the showrunner's opinion that prevails. Showrunners can vary greatly in demeanor and how much control they exert. But it's generally understood that, while the director is empowered in many significant ways, they, together with every department head, are ultimately serving the showrunner's vision. A director may help to *evolve* that vision, but usually not without the show-runner's consent.

As you might imagine, showrunning is a hellishly difficult, high-pressured job. Any decision affecting the episode you're directing can have a rippling effect on all episodes that follow. It's wise to remember that showrunners are usually concerned with many scripts at once. They are supervising the other writers — often rewriting their scripts — or writing episodes themselves. The showrunner is also likely to be supervising the editing of completed episodes and preparing them for delivery to the network or streaming service. If actors are concerned about the arc of their characters or the general direction of the story, they confer with the showrunner. When the show goes over budget, the showrunner may be asked to reconceive complicated sequences in order to shoot them less expensively. If an actor gets sick or turns out not to have chemistry with other cast members, the showrunner has to make changes and reimagine a complex puzzle, all while keeping the production train on track and on schedule.

In evaluating a director, showrunners will naturally ask themselves if that person will lighten their load or make their job more difficult. So it's best to treat your relationship to the showrunner with great care. The tone meeting is where you will get a chance to ask your questions regarding the dynamics of individual scenes, actors' strengths and weaknesses, and anything else on your mind. You will want to emerge from that meeting with a clear sense of the story and its deeper themes. This is helpful in its own right, but it can also go far to assure the showrunner that the episode is in good hands.

What I hope for in a showrunner is someone who respects the value directors can add to a project and doesn't overload them with too many particulars about how to achieve results. The best showrunners have an ability to convey important themes and subtext, and the sense to let directors bring their own creativity to the process. I prefer from the showrunner a "don't screw it up" attitude rather than micromanagement because the latter conveys distrust and can discourage the director from being adventurous. It's a little like knowing not to give line readings to actors: You may get the desired inflection for that particular moment, but you've risked discouraging the actor from trusting their own impulses.

Besides being, in a real sense, your boss, showrunners are also subject to the same frustrations and imperfect behavior we all are. It's helpful to keep in mind the considerable pressure on them, even while you're coping with your own stress. Ideally, you can find support from your showrunner. And if any of them are reading this, I'd suggest that a well-timed compliment can do wonders for your directors' spirits. But this often doesn't happen. Showrunners may be too busy putting out fires or preparing other scripts; they may be unsure whether you are delivering the episode they are hoping for, one on which their own job security may depend.

It's possible, and certainly desirable, for the relationship with your showrunner to be a partnership. As with other department heads with whom you work, you should take responsibility for developing trust. Be as prepared as you can whenever you speak to showrunners. Choose your questions carefully, both to honor their limited time and to convey that you won't be bothering them to solve things you can figure out yourself. I try to limit my questions either to tone and subtext or to the deeper thematic concerns that drive the episode. When other issues come up, stay mindful of whether or not they rise to the level of requiring the showrunner's input. I'm not suggesting you need to be shy or especially reluctant to engage the showrunner, but be aware of your own responsibilities. There is great subtlety in the dynamic between showrunner and director. It will probably only be through experience that you come to an understanding of what works best for you.

The director should make a priority of realizing the story points and character moments the showrunner wants delivered. The director can put a stamp on whether the storytelling is vibrant or mundane, but they must not change the story unless it's in consultation with the showrunner. If you feel you can improve something, great. But you must ask yourself if your approach might potentially be in conflict with the showrunner's intentions. Ideally, your choices are inspired by the elements you have inherited, but if you think you might be straying from the showrunner's ideas, you should seek approval for what you intend.

If you imagine a more interesting staging than what's on the page, or if you feel a problem can be solved by rewriting, the showrunner is the one who must approve the changes. Often, when you're considering asking for script adjustments, the writer or producer/director will approach the showrunner on your behalf. At times I prefer to make the approach myself, however, because it's an opportunity to discuss possible options. If there is simply too much work to fit into the schedule, I'll try to come up with my own suggestions as to how things might be shortened or condensed, at least to kick-start the discussion.

You will often watch auditions with the showrunner or a designated writer. Just as it is for you, the audition is your colleague's only chance to develop a feel for the performer. Most writers, even at this early stage, will respect your primary role in dealing with the actors and will wait for you to give any adjustments to them before they chime in. If the audition is for a recurring role, the showrunner will probably take the lead in the interview and audition for the sensible reason that they know better than you what is in store for the character. You will find that each situation requires a mutually respectful way of proceeding, and it's important, particularly for younger directors, not to shrink from your role. Your relationship with those who are cast begins here. It's helpful to get a sense of how you personally interact or engage with an actor you will be directing. When casting decisions are being made (and often this is based on recorded auditions only), make sure your voice is heard. You may not get all the choices you prefer, but generally, the showrunner will respect that it's you who will be charged with getting the performance. Your opinions will be given considerable weight. Be prepared to explain and defend your choices about whom you liked or didn't like because, ultimately, you will need the showrunner to sign off on who gets cast. You should assess how adamantly you feel in opposing a strong preference from the showrunner, though; even if you win your argument, you may have trouble overcoming the showrunner's first impression when they are evaluating your results. Don't back down easily from a strong instinct. But at the same time, remember that not all battles are of equal importance. There is give and take in most good relationships.

The showrunner will rarely be on set with you; most frequently, they will only be there for particularly significant scenes. In the absence of the showrunner, you will sometimes be joined at the video monitor by the writer of the episode. As long as professional responsibilities are clear, writers can be helpful in adding to your understanding of subtext and character. I'll often solicit the opinion of the writer about a particular take or performance because that input can help bring my own response into better focus. If the writer is overly anxious about particular beats being realized in a literal sense, exactly as they were discussed in the writers' room, their presence can be quite challenging. But most experienced writers are mindful of the director's process and the appropriate professional boundaries.

One of the sacrosanct responsibilities of the director is managing the actors' performances. Acting notes should always be delivered via the director unless that director has enlisted help from someone else. Seasoned writers and most showrunners generally understand this and are respectful of both the director's role and their challenges in getting the performance. Proper protocol is for writers to give directors any performance notes they may have so that they can be discussed and the director can consider how they might be translated to the actor.

When a writer gives me a note regarding an actor's performance, I measure it against my intentions for the scene. If the note occurs too early in the process, I may have to make clear that I'll need another take or two to get the scene closer to where I think it should be before evaluating changes, and after that we can consider a note more meaningfully. My own goals for the performance may in fact actually address the writer's concern. Or it might turn out that the note was prescient and fixes something I hadn't properly anticipated. I have found that this approach generally leads to consensus.

Yet disagreements do occur. I prefer to avoid confrontation when possible and consider it a challenge either to speak effectively against a note I feel is wrong or to figure out a way to address the writer's concern while still honoring my intentions for the scene. No director wants to, nor should, feel that they are simply there to relay directing choices made by others. But it bears repeating that a showrunner's wishes need to be respected. The challenge for a director can sometimes become how to incorporate a note in a way that maintains the director's own sense of integrity and does not conflict with their vision for how to tell the story.

The situation can be more challenging when the writer or showrunner wants to deliver a note directly to an actor. Showrunners (and often other writers) usually have a much longer history with the cast than does a director, who may have just been introduced to them and who will soon be gone. The showrunner has been a constant in the actors' lives and is usually the one to whom they turn to understand their characters or broader story arcs. In addition, good showrunners appreciate their cast's concerns and aspirations for their characters. This provides reassurance that there is a vision in place, and someone who will listen. It's understandable that, at times, the lines of authority may blur for writers who are used to engaging the actors in other contexts. It's also usually the case on a television series that actors want, ultimately, to please the showrunner; they're always eager to learn what that person's view for the scene might be. I'll often reinforce an adjustment I'm suggesting to an actor by invoking the showrunner as having agreed with the particular note I'm delivering. I don't mind that in doing so I might be diminishing my authority in the actor's eyes; I mainly care about getting the performance I want.

Most writers and showrunners are sensitive to all of this and recognize that their interference may undermine the director's authority. Less often understood is that such interference puts the actors in the difficult position of not knowing how to reconcile mixed messages. But whatever the case, it's important for you, as the director, to develop an ability to set effective boundaries in a way that will win you respect, not resentment.

I once directed a sequence during which the showrunner was watching rehearsal. I was trying to work on several things simultaneously: setting the blocking for the actors, arranging some critical background performances that contextualized the scene, and perfecting a camera move that would tell the story sequentially, without the necessity of an edit. After the first take, I walked onto the set to make my fixes, which first involved asking the dolly grip to delay the timing of a camera move that ended in the reveal of the lead actor. I then turned toward that actor and saw the showrunner with him, gesticulating while giving what appeared to be a performance note. I arrived as the showrunner exited and asked the actor what he had been told. I knew my very question was putting him in an awkward position of not wanting to offend either the showrunner or me. But I needed to know what the adjustment was — not just to have an opinion about it, but so I could consider how it might impact other things I was orchestrating.

If the showrunner had come to me with this particular note, I would have been grateful because, as it turned out, I instantly saw the wisdom of it. Yet the way he had acted was disrespectful and undermining of me as the director. It also affected the timing of the camera move I was setting and required me to make changes to it.

At the break, I told the showrunner simply that if he had performance notes in the future, I would appreciate his delivering them to me. The reason, I explained, was that it's my job to deal with the actors so that they are not potentially confused by being told different things by different people in authority. In addition, I must know what the actor is playing if I am to fold it into the fabric that is being woven by all the other story threads I'm handling. I mentioned previous other instances when he had expressed his feelings to me about particular scenes and reminded him that he had always been heard. If I had ignored those earlier notes, that would have occasioned a different discussion.

I try never to create any sort of impasse but to treat others with the same respect I want for myself. Fortunately, in this case, the showrunner apologized, never repeated the offense, and invited me back for future episodes. The relationship between director and showrunner can be complicated, primarily, I think, because both people want the same thing: the very best show possible. It can create bumps in the road when opinions differ on how to get there. But with mutual respect, the process of finding solutions is usually harmonious and creative, and the relationship can be a source of support for both showrunner and director.

CHAPTER FOURTEEN

INNER STATES

I WISH I COULD SAY IT WAS ONLY in my early days of directing that I was visited by feelings of inadequacy, fear of failure, or anxiety that the answers might not come. But truthfully, they seem to be a component of just about every job I do. Thankfully, I often also get to experience exhilaration, the joy of seeing the work come together, a sense of clarity and accomplishment, and appreciation for my collaborators. But the stakes can feel high, and doubt is very much a part of the process — or should be — as you try to tease something into existence that will be shared with and evaluated by your peers, your employer, and the viewing public.

The wide range of emotional and mental states that the demands of directing an episode of television can trigger is a challenge that often goes unacknowledged. You're creating an experience for others at the same time that you're likely discovering it for yourself. And you will usually be constrained by circumstances gone awry, budget concerns, and all the vagaries of production. But the clock is ticking, others are awaiting your decisions, and there is no turning back. One of my favorite directors, Francois Truffaut, made a film entitled *La Nuit Americaine* (*Day for Night*), which was about the production of a film. He included the sly twist of giving the character of the director (played by himself) a hearing aid, which enabled him to pretend not to hear questions he didn't know the answers to or preferred not to think about. It's easy to feel deluged by the onslaught of questions coming your way, and Truffaut depicted a fantasy many of us share — that it would be nice, sometimes, simply to tune it all out. But the reality is that the director is the one person who can never be missing in action.

Learning to deal with the emotional rollercoaster you're likely to experience as a director is pretty much a requirement for doing a good job, and not just for your own peace of mind. You have been given a great opportunity with enormous responsibilities, one of which is to lead. There are a few inner qualities to cultivate that, in my experience, are vital to success. (At the very least, they can be helpful in preventing conditions from deteriorating.) An ability to prioritize all the things demanding your attention is one of the most important of those qualities. It's easy to get hijacked by worries about how you will be judged or by distractions from the main thread of your story. Staying focused on effectively delivering your vision takes a special kind of awareness. It requires being mindful.

Simply defined, to be mindful is to stay as aware as possible of all that is happening within you, emotionally, physically, and mentally. Rather than being lost in thoughts, feelings, or sensations, you develop a sort of witness state. From this perspective, you're better able to objectively consider how to navigate through difficult situations and artistic challenges. You're more likely to be fully present in the moment-to-moment decisions that a director must make almost continually. A meditation practice can be very helpful in developing this muscle. I've had one for a long time, and I can tell you — it's called a practice because that's what it takes.

Mindful awareness is difficult to maintain. Much of the time, I'm aware of failing at it miserably, which is a kind of mindfulness itself, I guess. We're all human, and therefore subject to being carried away by longings, anxieties, ambitions, desires, hurt feelings ... the full catastrophe, as Zorba the Greek described it. The job of directing can invite an obsessiveness that complicates the challenge. When you're in the throes of bringing something new into being — based upon a vision you have or are trying to evolve — it's easy to ignore the reality right around you. I remember, years ago, being shocked to learn that a director had been killed because he exited his camera helicopter and walked straight into the still-spinning propeller. God only knows what directing problem he may have been obsessing about.

I'll often feel the need, when directing, to pare away distractions simply to stay mindful of my purpose, shutting out anything that distracts me from it. When feeling under the gun, this narrowed focus is quite essential. But it carries the risk that we may miss opportunities by not staying open enough, or that we defeat our purpose by failing to be fully present with our collaborators. Once, my lack of presence almost cost me dearly.

I had just finished directing my first episode of a show I greatly admired. It had gone very well, I thought, and I was surprised when I didn't hear from the producers as they scheduled directors for the following season. Since I very much wanted to return and thought they'd been happy with my work, I called to inquire. I was told that "number one" on the call sheet — the lead actor — had taken offense to something I had done and would prefer I not return. Apparently, I had "laid hands" on him once during rehearsal to move him a short distance to where I wanted him "marked." (That's the place where tape is put on the floor to indicate where the actors stand during rehearsal so that their positions may be properly lit.)

I felt mortified and actually confused since I remembered only countless intimate discussions with that actor exploring the particulars of each scene. Then I recalled where my offense probably occurred. It's funny how conveniently I'd blocked this memory. It was in a low-light situation involving five actors in a tight space at a tense, critical moment in the story. Framing the image to include only the specific cast I wanted each shot to include was precise and challenging. On top of that, the day before had been uncharacteristically difficult between my cameraman and me, and he and I were not working together as smoothly as I would have liked. In fact, I was still upset not to have gotten the previous day's work exactly as I'd wanted and was holding on to some resentment about that, not terribly interested in my own part in the miscommunication. I recalled that, when staging the scene, I'd felt beleaguered, reluctant to trust others, unmindful of those around me. I couldn't be sure I hadn't (and actually, I think I had) forcibly moved the actors a few inches either way to get the precise positioning I wanted. It was a situation that can easily occur on a shoot when one has trouble letting go of distracting concerns and acts thoughtlessly.

I asked the producers to approach the actor and to express both my deep regret and my sincere desire to return to work with him again. I considered him a terrific talent and hated leaving him with an impression so at odds with my values for myself. I was relieved when they got back to me with the news that he had relented and I would get another episode to direct in the coming season.

When the new season was in progress several months later, I returned to start preparing my episode. I knew myself well enough to realize that I'd be distracted until I made sure personally to mend fences with the leading actor and regain his goodwill. So, on the first day of my prep, I broke away to seek him out and ask if I might have a word with him. I told him I wanted to apologize. He seemed to have no idea what I was talking about.

"For what?" he asked.

"Well," I answered, in my best attempt to mix humor with explanation while not fanning another possible fire, "as I understand it, I apparently mistook you for a dance partner."

His face expressed pure bewilderment. I could only think to add that perhaps I was under a mistaken impression, but that I wanted to assure him that I had only the greatest respect for him, both personally and as an actor. I promised that in the future I would always be sure to approach him more professionally and with the appreciation I truly have for the actor's art.

We went on in the episode to have an enjoyable working relationship, as we did on several more episodes in subsequent seasons. I think it's fair to say we actually became friends.

Two or three years later, this actor had the opportunity to direct an episode of the show himself, and I made sure to offer whatever counsel I could as he went through the experience. I was preparing another episode while he was in the middle of shooting his when, one day, he sought me out, practically buzzing with energy and amusement.

"Dan!" he said. "I need to tell you something!" He continued, "You remember that nonsense a few years ago when I got so offended because you physically moved me a few inches when we were rehearsing?"

"Yes?" I asked, not sure where this was going, as this was the first time he had ever acknowledged any such offense had taken place.

"Well, I just did the same thing when I was directing the guest star last night! I thought, God! I totally get how completely absorbed you become when directing, and I knew I had to tell you!"

We laughed, but he had learned something illuminating about the directing process. Trying to make the best possible episode, a director can be so focused that they forget the need for normal courtesies. In trying to access your deepest creative resources, it can at times seem almost as if you've entered another world. But the reality is you haven't left this one, and so you would do well to remember its rules.

This experience reminds me of the importance of staying self-aware and not venting about the all-too-human frustrations that inevitably occur while directing; not just because that should never be an excuse for bad behavior, but because the director occupies an elevated position. While you probably experience yourself as the flawed human being that you are, the fact is that, while directing, you're in a position of authority. You may have power over another person's sense of job security or even self-worth. Mindfulness at the moment I had felt the impulse to move the actor like a chess piece would have given me the opportunity to better assess the less-than-ideal state I was in and to choose not to act from it. As you occupy the role of director, an important fact to remember is that, no matter what you're weathering internally, you're best served if you embrace the reality that you are the leader.

Managing your inner states is vital because good leaders should not create chaos by erratic decision making, nor generate a void by withdrawing into themselves. With all of the emotional and mental challenges the director has to face, it's essential to find the will to take ownership of the leadership role. In my experience, that does not mean projecting false confidence, although in truth that can sometimes get you through a rough patch. More often it's a better plan to admit what you haven't yet figured out and be open to the ideas of others. That doesn't mean you're weak, or that you lack confidence. I sometimes like to turn to writers or script supervisors who may be with me at the monitor and ask for their feelings about a particular take. I'm not obliged to agree with them, but often it helps clarify my own feelings, ironically even if I disagree with them.

Filmmaking is a uniquely collaborative art, and I have been assisted countless times by others contributing their expertise or intuitive solutions to a creative problem. The best leader on a film set, I believe, is one who creates an environment where others are invited to contribute their ideas and feel respected for the effort. Leadership also requires, however, that you be secure enough in your power to take suggestions *and* not to take them. When the efforts of others help you to get what you want, or perhaps improve upon what you had imagined, an expression of gratitude goes a long way toward encouraging the best efforts of everyone. It also makes for a more rewarding and enjoyable experience on the set, which should always be a priority whenever possible. This is especially true when hours have been long or the physical conditions of production challenging. It's very common for cast and crew alike to become mentally taxed, so it's a good idea to remind yourself how hard other people are working for and alongside you.

There are other styles of leadership that aren't so open to inclusion, and it's true that there will be occasions when there simply isn't time for soliciting opinions. But in my experience, it's more rewarding to lead in this way. It can lessen stress if you hold onto awareness that you don't have to face everything alone. Plus, input from other talented people will often yield better results.

There is, however, a unifying feature in effective leaders of all stripes, and that is a sense of command. This is not to say that a director needs to be *commanding*. But people need to sense the seriousness and purposefulness of the director's intent and know that they are wholly committed to delivering a vision, and to do so within the time allotted. Fiercely committed, even. I think most casts and crews will line up behind any director who they feel has fully accepted responsibility for the project, and who expects a similar commitment from them. You can always tell when you're on a set where the director has not stepped into that role: There is a lack of urgency and purpose, and a void created by no one truly being in charge. I think this happens when the director succumbs to a desire to be rescued by others — not unusual in the heat of the moment to *feel*, perhaps, but a mistake to give in to.

A quality that can contribute to a sense of command is what I would call presence. That word has several meanings, but the one that applies here has to do with an ability to be with yourself at a deep level, in contact with what I sometimes think of as a still center within. Your collaborators need to know that within you, there is a *there* there. You benefit from experiencing that center, as well; it puts you in touch with your true feelings about creative questions. It can even provide you with a path to the meaning of a story moment that is eluding you. When you're in that state of presence, you're focused, patient, and alert. You're serving something other than your ego: You're serving story.

This requires a willingness to believe in inner resources that arise when you have an intention and put yourself in a receptive, open state. I'm not saying one need be serene and in control of one's impulses at all times. I've never managed that for anything close to a whole episode, and certainly not throughout shooting, which can be very stressful. My personal outlet is often to pace while I wait for the assistant director to call out, "Ready!" It's quite normal to feel pressure, stress, or anxiety in moments when you don't know the answer to what might jumpstart a performance or how to consolidate shots to get everything you need. But if you can find, even momentarily, that still place within, you have a better chance of receiving the answers you seek. Stress may be unavoidable, but I can pretty much guarantee it compromises your ability to do your best work. Finding a state of presence involves penetrating to a deeper layer of experience, rather like diving beneath storm-driven seas and discovering the calm waters below. It can give you a moment's clarity, which sometimes is all you need.

Often, the first step to finding this state is simply to become present to what is around you and not to get lost in preconceptions about how you imagine things might go. There's a sign in some gambling halls or bingo parlors that says, "You have to be present to win." I think that about says it. You have to be present to the reality in front of you to respond with appropriateness, specificity, and sometimes opportunism if you're going to guide the story through to its best incarnation. There is an often repeated Latin phrase, *festina lente*, that translates as "make haste slowly." Even when there is a need to hurry, you mustn't get ahead of yourself, nor leave others behind.

Early in my career, I thought not being sure of myself was a sign of weakness or incompetence. I've come to appreciate that the people who are the best at what they do are often the ones quickest to acknowledge what they don't know. This makes real knowing possible. Eastern spiritual traditions refer to a certain open attitude as "beginner's mind." One way I understand this is that learning can only occur when one is in a state of openness and not knowing, being present to what is unfolding. Creativity involves bringing into being something that did not exist before. Our job really is to stay curious and to evaluate whether or not what emerges from our imaginations — and the imaginations of our collaborators — feels right and contributes to the vitality of our story. The real achievement, I think, is developing the mindset to stay open to what presents itself, even when it appears in the shape of an insoluble problem, and to trust that your inner resources and those of your collaborators will lead to a solution.

There's much to figure out in this job: how to define the story so that we care deeply about it, how best to fashion the way information is communicated, what strategies might yield desired results. But what we sometimes miss is how much simply arises and waits for us to recognize it. So then, who is doing the creating? We'd like to think it's our own brilliance and talent. Our egos come in after the fact and claim all the credit, but in truth the ego wasn't the part of ourselves that produced the work. Inspiration comes from a realm that we do not control, usually when we stay receptive and hold honest intent. The skill is often in determining what are the right questions to ask. I find that they usually originate from that still center, if we only slow down and check in with ourselves to identify them: "Why did that particular detail draw my attention? What is it opening up for me? How does it make me feel?" The surprising insight we hope to receive must be invited, and we must be open in order to recognize when it arrives.

CHAPTER FIFTEEN

WRAPPING UP

THE JOB OF GUEST DIRECTOR IN SERIES television often feels like trying to make as good a version as possible of somebody else's show. Though I've emphasized throughout these pages how important it is to take ownership and responsibility as the storyteller, few people outside the business understand how crucial your role is, how much you are actually responsible for the moment-to-moment storytelling, and how vital your contribution is to the *meaning* and the *experience* of the episode. But recognition aside, and despite all the givens you inherit, the answer to "how creative can the episodic director be?" is: very.

By staying open and committed to making things *work*, the series-television director sometimes gains access to creative solutions that emerge from sheer determination. I'm not suggesting that it's always possible to overcome a weak script on a bad television show with poor actors. But even on good shows, there inevitably are sequences that stubbornly resist all efforts to bring them to life. I've shared some of my experiences in which new and deeper meanings arose precisely because I *couldn't* get the rewrites I wanted and had to seek other solutions.

You're in the process of finding and shaping your episode's story from the moment you start to form impressions in prep, all the way through the delivery of your cut. The director's cut is the edited version of your show and the product of your work with the editor — another in a long list of collaborators whose skillset can be a great support to you. I haven't focused much on the nuances of editing, but this is a crucial part of the process. Be sure to take advantage of the time afforded to you in the editing room; the impact of your episode greatly depends on the way it's pieced together. You have the opportunity to perfect the performances and determine the way the story is told, moment to moment. No one can watch the show until your cut is delivered, guaranteeing that the producers' first viewing will reflect how you feel the show works best.

After delivering the director's cut, the series director's role is at best advisory, and usually not even that. The showrunner — generally in consultation with the network, cable outlet, or streaming service — has the authority to do with the episode what they like. Your work is essentially done, and you're in the position of hoping that the showrunner will either agree with your choices or find ways to improve upon them. While your role as episodic director may not bring you the recognition you might like for the creative role you play, increasingly, the job is being acknowledged for how critical it is to an episode's overall quality.

The good news is that there are better things than recognition, and this job has the potential to provide them: the feeling of being alive to the inner gifts that come through you and the joy of sharing with others what you find to be authentic and most deeply true. If you ask me, not much can top that.

AFTERWORD

EARLY IN MY CAREER, I HAD THE privilege of shadowing Dan Attias while he directed an episode of *The Americans*. I had shadowed other directors numerous times on other shows, never getting much closer to that first opportunity to direct an episode. But the experience with Dan was a revelation and a turning point.

Before moving to Los Angeles, I had lived in Ireland off and on for ten years, directing commercials and narrative films. But, as Dan explains here in detail, series television presents its own challenges. There was a lot to learn as I tried to make the transition to TV, and I relished the opportunity of having a front-row seat to observe the skills and instincts that make Dan such an accomplished talent. It's not surprising that he is often asked to take on the most challenging episodes of a series because he seems always to deliver beautiful work while presiding over a smoothly run set.

The first quality I noticed about Dan was his boundless positive energy. Directing involves endless problem solving, which he always undertook with a sense of adventure and possibility. On location scouts, if a choice piqued his interest, Dan would be laser-focused, assessing its potential and walking through the scene, sometimes literally acting it out. And if I were lucky, he would ask me to stand in for one actor or another as he evolved his plans. Once shooting began, I felt his excitement when he would hit on just the right way to stage a scene, or when an actor brought vibrancy and depth to the performance.

As I scribbled notes while watching Dan direct, or after he'd given me a gem of advice, I wondered how many other aspiring TV directors were getting chances like this, chances to be exposed to this level of expertise and mastery. The longer I work in television, the more I understand how rare an opportunity I had and how few other young directors get to enjoy this level of mentorship. I am thrilled Dan has decided to put his approach to directing and storytelling in book form, and has done so with such eloquence and thoughtfulness that, as I read, I feel again like I am sitting in the director's chair beside him, taking in lesson after lesson.

Dan also firmly believes the industry must become more inclusive and has actively championed minority and female directors, myself included, inviting underrepresented aspiring directors to his sets before there were programs or incentives to do so. This is because Dan is not only a great director but is also a natural educator. When I shadowed him, he would often share with me his thought process, much as he does in this book. I can smile now at the ways I have absorbed into my own process what he taught and modeled — how many times I've solved what seemed unsolvable, or worked with a showrunner to find creative solutions to a story or scheduling problem. Just how much of Dan's practical and creative advice has helped me in my day-to-day work life is remarkable. I hope you have found Dan's wisdom as powerful as I have.

Steph Green
Emmy-nominated director whose credits include *The Mandalorian*, *Watchmen*, *The Americans*, *Billions*, and *The Deuce*.

ACKNOWLEDGMENTS

I AM VERY GRATEFUL TO ALL THE YOUNG directors whom I have been privileged to mentor and who started me on the road to sharing my process, a journey that led eventually to this book. Thanks are due to two of those mentees in particular — Max Joseph and Steph Green — for reading the manuscript and offering me their insights.

Thanks also to Laurie Winer and Karen Krumpak, whose editorial suggestions significantly clarified the material, and to Robert Abele, whose interview with me for the *DGA Quarterly* first inspired me to consider writing about directing. He was very helpful and encouraging in the early stages of the book. Seth Greenland and Eric Roth also provided valuable feedback.

Special thanks to my wife, Diana, whose careful reading contributed at every stage of my writing process, and whose enthusiasm was an inspiration to keep going.

ABOUT THE AUTHOR

Dan Attias has worked as a director in the film and television industry since 1984. As a director of series television, he has received the Directors Guild of America award for outstanding direction of dramatic television for *The Wire* and has been nominated for episodes of *The Sopranos, Six Feet Under, Homeland,* and *The Marvelous Mrs. Maisel.* He has received Emmy award nominations for his comedy directing on *Entourage* and continues to work on some of the most celebrated American television shows. His other credits include *The Americans, Deadwood, True Blood, Lost, Big Love, The Killing, True Detective, The Walking Dead, Bloodline, Friday Night Lights, It's Always Sunny in Philadelphia, Seven Seconds, Billions,* and *The Boys.*

Dan started his career by studying acting, then worked as an assistant director on *E.T. the Extra-terrestrial, Airplane!, One From the Heart,* and several other feature films. He has taught acting and directing workshops in the United States and has conducted master classes in Italy, Greece, Brazil, Mexico, and Canada. He has also mentored many young directors, several of whom have gone on to successful careers in television. For more information, visit DanAttias.com.

MICHAEL WIESE PRODUCTIONS

IN A DARK TIME, a light bringer came along, leading the curious and the frustrated to clarity and empowerment. It took the well-guarded secrets out of the hands of the few and made them available to all. It spread a spirit of openness and creative freedom, and built a storehouse of knowledge dedicated to the betterment of the arts.

The essence of Michael Wiese Productions (MWP) is empowering people who have the burning desire to express themselves creatively. We help them realize their dreams by putting the tools in their hands. We demystify the sometimes secretive worlds of screenwriting, directing, acting, producing, film financing, and other media crafts.

By doing so, we hope to bring forth a realization of 'conscious media,' which we define as being positively charged, emphasizing hope, and affirming positive values like trust, cooperation, self-empowerment, freedom, and love. Grounded in the deep roots of myth, it aims to be healing both for those who make the art and those who encounter it. It hopes to be transformative for people, opening doors to new possibilities and pulling back veils to reveal hidden worlds.

MWP has built a storehouse of knowledge unequaled in the world, for no other publisher has so many titles on the media arts. Please visit www.mwp.com, where you will find many free resources and a 25% discount on our books. Sign up and become part of the wider creative community!

MICHAEL WIESE, Co-Publisher
GERALDINE OVERTON, Co-Publisher